Connected Mathematics 2

How Likely Is It?

Understanding Probability

Glenda Lappan

James T. Fey

William M. Fitzgerald

Susan N. Friel

Elizabeth Difanis Phillips

PEARSON

Boston, Massachusetts · Glenview, Illinois · Shoreview, Minnesota · Upper Saddle River, New Jersey

Connected Mathematics™ was developed at Michigan State University with financial support from the Michigan State University Office of the Provost, Computing and Technology, and the College of Natural Science.

This material is based upon work supported by the National Science Foundation under Grant No. MDR 9150217 and Grant No. ESI 9986372. Opinions expressed are those of the authors and not necessarily those of the Foundation.

The Michigan State University authors and administration have agreed that all MSU royalties arising from this publication will be devoted to purposes supported by the MSU Mathematics Education Enrichment Fund.

Acknowledgments appear on page 79, which constitutes an extension of this copyright page.

13-digit ISBN 978-0-13-366135-4
10-digit ISBN 0-13-366135-0
5 6 7 8 9 10 V003 11 10

Authors of Connected Mathematics

(from left to right) Glenda Lappan, Betty Phillips, Susan Friel, Bill Fitzgerald, Jim Fey

Glenda Lappan is a University Distinguished Professor in the Department of Mathematics at Michigan State University. Her research and development interests are in the connected areas of students' learning of mathematics and mathematics teachers' professional growth and change related to the development and enactment of K–12 curriculum materials.

James T. Fey is a Professor of Curriculum and Instruction and Mathematics at the University of Maryland. His consistent professional interest has been development and research focused on curriculum materials that engage middle and high school students in problem-based collaborative investigations of mathematical ideas and their applications.

William M. Fitzgerald (*Deceased*) was a Professor in the Department of Mathematics at Michigan State University. His early research was on the use of concrete materials in supporting student learning and led to the development of teaching materials for laboratory environments. Later he helped develop a teaching model to support student experimentation with mathematics.

Susan N. Friel is a Professor of Mathematics Education in the School of Education at the University of North Carolina at Chapel Hill. Her research interests focus on statistics education for middle-grade students and, more broadly, on teachers' professional development and growth in teaching mathematics K–8.

Elizabeth Difanis Phillips is a Senior Academic Specialist in the Mathematics Department of Michigan State University. She is interested in teaching and learning mathematics for both teachers and students. These interests have led to curriculum and professional development projects at the middle school and high school levels, as well as projects related to the teaching and learning of algebra across the grades.

Field Test Sites for CMP2

During the development of the revised edition of *Connected Mathematics* (CMP2), more than 100 classroom teachers have field-tested materials at 49 school sites in 12 states and the District of Columbia. This classroom testing occurred over three academic years (2001 through 2004), allowing careful study of the effectiveness of each of the 24 units that comprise the program. A special thanks to the students and teachers at these pilot schools.

Arkansas

Magnolia Public Schools
Kittena Bell*, Judith Trowell*; *Central Elementary School:* Maxine Broom, Betty Eddy, Tiffany Fallin, Bonnie Flurry, Carolyn Monk, Elizabeth Tye; *Magnolia Junior High School:* Monique Bryan, Ginger Cook, David Graham, Shelby Lamkin

Colorado

Boulder Public Schools
Nevin Platt Middle School: Judith Koenig

St. Vrain Valley School District, Longmont
Westview Middle School: Colleen Beyer, Kitty Canupp, Ellie Decker*, Peggy McCarthy, Tanya deNobrega, Cindy Payne, Ericka Pilon, Andrew Roberts

District of Columbia

Capitol Hill Day School: Ann Lawrence

Georgia

University of Georgia, Athens
Brad Findell

Madison Public Schools
Morgan County Middle School: Renee Burgdorf, Lynn Harris, Nancy Kurtz, Carolyn Stewart

Maine

Falmouth Public Schools
Falmouth Middle School: Donna Erikson, Joyce Hebert, Paula Hodgkins, Rick Hogan, David Legere, Cynthia Martin, Barbara Stiles, Shawn Towle*

Michigan

Portland Public Schools
Portland Middle School: Mark Braun, Holly DeRosia, Kathy Dole*, Angie Foote, Teri Keusch, Tammi Wardwell

Traverse City Area Public Schools
Bertha Vos Elementary: Kristin Sak; *Central Grade School:* Michelle Clark; Jody Meyers; *Eastern Elementary:* Karrie Tufts; *Interlochen Elementary:* Mary McGee-Cullen; *Long Lake Elementary:* Julie Faulkner*, Charlie Maxbauer, Katherine Sleder; *Norris Elementary:* Hope Slanaker; *Oak Park Elementary:* Jessica Steed; *Traverse Heights Elementary:* Jennifer Wolfert; *Westwoods Elementary:* Nancy Conn; *Old Mission Peninsula School:* Deb Larimer; *Traverse City East Junior High:* Ivanka Berkshire, Ruthanne Kladder, Jan Palkowski, Jane Peterson, Mary Beth Schmitt; *Traverse City West Junior High:* Dan Fouch*, Ray Fouch

Sturgis Public Schools
Sturgis Middle School: Ellen Eisele

Minnesota

Burnsville School District 191
Hidden Valley Elementary: Stephanie Cin, Jane McDevitt

Hopkins School District 270
Alice Smith Elementary: Sandra Cowing, Kathleen Gustafson, Martha Mason, Scott Stillman; *Eisenhower Elementary:* Chad Bellig, Patrick Berger, Nancy Glades, Kye Johnson, Shane Wasserman, Victoria Wilson; *Gatewood Elementary:* Sarah Ham, Julie Kloos, Janine Pung, Larry Wade; *Glen Lake Elementary:* Jacqueline Cramer, Kathy Hering, Cecelia Morris,

Robb Trenda; *Katherine Curren Elementary:* Diane Bancroft, Sue DeWit, John Wilson; *L. H. Tanglen Elementary:* Kevin Athmann, Lisa Becker, Mary LaBelle, Kathy Rezac, Roberta Severson; *Meadowbrook Elementary:* Jan Gauger, Hildy Shank, Jessica Zimmerman; *North Junior High:* Laurel Hahn, Kristin Lee, Jodi Markuson, Bruce Mestemacher, Laurel Miller, Bonnie Rinker, Jeannine Salzer, Sarah Shafer, Cam Stottler; *West Junior High:* Alicia Beebe, Kristie Earl, Nobu Fujii, Pam Georgetti, Susan Gilbert, Regina Nelson Johnson, Debra Lindstrom, Michele Luke*, Jon Sorenson

Minneapolis School District 1
Ann Sullivan K-8 School: Bronwyn Collins; Anne Bartel* (Curriculum and Instruction Office)

Wayzata School District 284
Central Middle School: Sarajane Myers, Dan Nielsen, Tanya Ravenholdt

White Bear Lake School District 624
Central Middle School: Amy Jorgenson, Michelle Reich, Brenda Sammon

New York

New York City Public Schools
IS 89: Yelena Aynbinder, Chi-Man Ng, Nina Rapaport, Joel Spengler, Phyllis Tam*, Brent Wyso; *Wagner Middle School:* Jason Appel, Intissar Fernandez, Yee Gee Get, Richard Goldstein, Irving Marcus, Sue Norton, Bernadita Owens, Jennifer Rehn*, Kevin Yuhas

---

* indicates a Field Test Site Coordinator

Ohio
Talawanda School District, Oxford
Talawanda Middle School: Teresa Abrams, Larry Brock, Heather Brosey, Julie Churchman, Monna Even, Karen Fitch, Bob George, Amanda Klee, Pat Meade, Sandy Montgomery, Barbara Sherman, Lauren Steidl

Miami University
Jeffrey Wanko*

Springfield Public Schools
Rockway School: Jim Mamer

Pennsylvania
Pittsburgh Public Schools
Kenneth Labuskes, Marianne O'Connor, Mary Lynn Raith*; *Arthur J. Rooney Middle School:* David Hairston, Stamatina Mousetis, Alfredo Zangaro; *Frick International Studies Academy:* Suzanne Berry, Janet Falkowski, Constance Finseth, Romika Hodge, Frank Machi; *Reizenstein Middle School:* Jeff Baldwin, James Brautigam, Lorena Burnett, Glen Cobbett, Michael Jordan, Margaret Lazur, Melissa Munnell, Holly Neely, Ingrid Reed, Dennis Reft

Texas
Austin Independent School District
Bedichek Middle School: Lisa Brown, Jennifer Glasscock, Vicki Massey

El Paso Independent School District
Cordova Middle School: Armando Aguirre, Anneliesa Durkes, Sylvia Guzman, Pat Holguin*, William Holguin, Nancy Nava, Laura Orozco, Michelle Peña, Roberta Rosen, Patsy Smith, Jeremy Wolf

Plano Independent School District
Patt Henry, James Wohlgehagen*; *Frankford Middle School:* Mandy Baker, Cheryl Butsch, Amy Dudley, Betsy Eshelman, Janet Greene, Cort Haynes, Kathy Letchworth, Kay Marshall, Kelly McCants, Amy Reck, Judy Scott, Syndy Snyder, Lisa Wang; *Wilson Middle School:* Darcie Bane, Amanda Bedenko, Whitney Evans, Tonelli Hatley, Sarah (Becky) Higgs, Kelly Johnston, Rebecca McElligott, Kay Neuse, Cheri Slocum, Kelli Straight

Washington
Evergreen School District
Shahala Middle School: Nicole Abrahamsen, Terry Coon*, Carey Doyle, Sheryl Drechsler, George Gemma, Gina Helland, Amy Hilario, Darla Lidyard, Sean McCarthy, Tilly Meyer, Willow Neuwelt, Todd Parsons, Brian Pederson, Stan Posey, Shawn Scott, Craig Sjoberg, Lynette Sundstrom, Charles Switzer, Luke Youngblood

Wisconsin
Beaver Dam Unified School District
Beaver Dam Middle School: Jim Braemer, Jeanne Frick, Jessica Greatens, Barbara Link, Dennis McCormick, Karen Michels, Nancy Nichols*, Nancy Palm, Shelly Stelsel, Susan Wiggins

---

* indicates a Field Test Site Coordinator

Reviews of CMP to Guide Development of CMP2

Before writing for CMP2 began or field tests were conducted, the first edition of *Connected Mathematics* was submitted to the mathematics faculties of school districts from many parts of the country and to 80 individual reviewers for extensive comments.

School District Survey Reviews of CMP

Arizona
Madison School District #38 (Phoenix)

Arkansas
Cabot School District, Little Rock School District, Magnolia School District

California
Los Angeles Unified School District

Colorado
St. Vrain Valley School District (Longmont)

Florida
Leon County Schools (Tallahassee)

Illinois
School District #21 (Wheeling)

Indiana
Joseph L. Block Junior High (East Chicago)

Kentucky
Fayette County Public Schools (Lexington)

Maine
Selection of Schools

Massachusetts
Selection of Schools

Michigan
Sparta Area Schools

Minnesota
Hopkins School District

Texas
Austin Independent School District, The El Paso Collaborative for Academic Excellence, Plano Independent School District

Wisconsin
Platteville Middle School

Individual Reviewers of CMP

Arkansas
Deborah Cramer; Robby Frizzell *(Taylor)*; Lowell Lynde *(University of Arkansas, Monticello)*; Leigh Manzer *(Norfork)*; Lynne Roberts *(Emerson High School, Emerson)*; Tony Timms *(Cabot Public Schools)*; Judith Trowell *(Arkansas Department of Higher Education)*

California
José Alcantar *(Gilroy)*; Eugenie Belcher *(Gilroy)*; Marian Pasternack *(Lowman M. S. T. Center, North Hollywood)*; Susana Pezoa *(San Jose)*; Todd Rabusin *(Hollister)*; Margaret Siegfried *(Ocala Middle School, San Jose)*; Polly Underwood *(Ocala Middle School, San Jose)*

Colorado
Janeane Golliher *(St. Vrain Valley School District, Longmont)*; Judith Koenig *(Nevin Platt Middle School, Boulder)*

Florida
Paige Loggins *(Swift Creek Middle School, Tallahassee)*

Illinois
Jan Robinson *(School District #21, Wheeling)*

Indiana
Frances Jackson *(Joseph L. Block Junior High, East Chicago)*

Kentucky
Natalee Feese *(Fayette County Public Schools, Lexington)*

Maine
Betsy Berry *(Maine Math & Science Alliance, Augusta)*

Maryland
Joseph Gagnon *(University of Maryland, College Park)*; Paula Maccini *(University of Maryland, College Park)*

Massachusetts
George Cobb *(Mt. Holyoke College, South Hadley)*; Cliff Kanold *(University of Massachusetts, Amherst)*

Michigan
Mary Bouck *(Farwell Area Schools)*; Carol Dorer *(Slauson Middle School, Ann Arbor)*; Carrie Heaney *(Forsythe Middle School, Ann Arbor)*; Ellen Hopkins *(Clague Middle School, Ann Arbor)*; Teri Keusch *(Portland Middle School, Portland)*; Valerie Mills *(Oakland Schools, Waterford)*; Mary Beth Schmitt *(Traverse City East Junior High, Traverse City)*; Jack Smith *(Michigan State University, East Lansing)*; Rebecca Spencer *(Sparta Middle School, Sparta)*; Ann Marie Nicoll Turner *(Tappan Middle School, Ann Arbor)*; Scott Turner *(Scarlett Middle School, Ann Arbor)*

Minnesota
Margarita Alvarez *(Olson Middle School, Minneapolis)*; Jane Amundson *(Nicollet Junior High, Burnsville)*; Anne Bartel *(Minneapolis Public Schools)*; Gwen Ranzau Campbell *(Sunrise Park Middle School, White Bear Lake)*; Stephanie Cin *(Hidden Valley Elementary, Burnsville)*; Joan Garfield *(University of Minnesota, Minneapolis)*; Gretchen Hall *(Richfield Middle School, Richfield)*; Jennifer Larson *(Olson Middle School, Minneapolis)*; Michele Luke *(West Junior High, Minnetonka)*; Jeni Meyer *(Richfield Junior High, Richfield)*; Judy Pfingsten *(Inver Grove Heights Middle School, Inver Grove Heights)*; Sarah Shafer *(North Junior High, Minnetonka)*; Genni Steele *(Central Middle School, White Bear Lake)*; Victoria Wilson *(Eisenhower Elementary, Hopkins)*; Paul Zorn *(St. Olaf College, Northfield)*

New York
Debra Altenau-Bartolino *(Greenwich Village Middle School, New York)*; Doug Clements *(University of Buffalo)*; Francis Curcio *(New York University, New York)*; Christine Dorosh *(Clinton School for Writers, Brooklyn)*; Jennifer Rehn *(East Side Middle School, New York)*; Phyllis Tam *(IS 89 Lab School, New York)*;

Marie Turini *(Louis Armstrong Middle School, New York)*; Lucy West *(Community School District 2, New York)*; Monica Witt *(Simon Baruch Intermediate School 104, New York)*

Pennsylvania
Robert Aglietti *(Pittsburgh)*; Sharon Mihalich *(Pittsburgh)*; Jennifer Plumb *(South Hills Middle School, Pittsburgh)*; Mary Lynn Raith *(Pittsburgh Public Schools)*

Texas
Michelle Bittick *(Austin Independent School District)*; Margaret Cregg *(Plano Independent School District)*; Sheila Cunningham *(Klein Independent School District)*; Judy Hill *(Austin Independent School District)*; Patricia Holguin *(El Paso Independent School District)*; Bonnie McNemar *(Arlington)*; Kay Neuse *(Plano Independent School District)*; Joyce Polanco *(Austin Independent School District)*; Marge Ramirez *(University of Texas at El Paso)*; Pat Rossman *(Baker Campus, Austin)*; Cindy Schimek *(Houston)*; Cynthia Schneider *(Charles A. Dana Center, University of Texas at Austin)*; Uri Treisman *(Charles A. Dana Center, University of Texas at Austin)*; Jacqueline Weilmuenster *(Grapevine-Colleyville Independent School District)*; LuAnn Weynand *(San Antonio)*; Carmen Whitman *(Austin Independent School District)*; James Wohlgehagen *(Plano Independent School District)*

Washington
Ramesh Gangolli *(University of Washington, Seattle)*

Wisconsin
Susan Lamon *(Marquette University, Hales Corner)*; Steve Reinhart *(retired, Chippewa Falls Middle School, Eau Claire)*

Table of Contents

How Likely Is It?
Understanding Probability

How Likely Is It?

You are on a game show. The host is holding a bucket with red, yellow, and blue blocks. You cannot see the blocks. Guess a color and then choose a block from the bucket. A player who correctly predicts the color of the block wins $500. After each selection, the block is returned to the bucket. What are your chances of winning the game?

You have a scratch-off prize card with five spots. Each spot covers the name of a prize. Two of the prizes match. You scratch off only two spots. If the prize under both spots match, you win. How likely is it that you will win?

Some people can curl their tongues into a "U" shape. Other people can't. What are the chances that a person can curl her or his tongue?

How do you make decisions? Suppose you are deciding whether to wear a raincoat. Would you ask "How likely is it that it will rain today?" Suppose you are deciding whether to buy a raffle ticket. Would you ask "What are the chances that I will win the raffle?" These questions ask about the probability that an event will occur.

Finding probabilities can help you understand past events. They can also help you make decisions about future events. In this unit, you will look at questions that involve probability, including the three questions on the opposite page.

Mathematical Highlights

Understanding Probability

In *How Likely Is It?*, you will explore concepts related to chance, or probability. You will analyze situations that have uncertain outcomes.

You will learn how to

- Use probabilities to predict what will happen over the long run

- Use the concepts of *equally likely* and *not equally likely*

- Analyze a game to see if it is fair (Does each player have an equal chance of winning?)

- Build two kinds of probability models:
  (1) Gather data from experiments (experimental probability)
  (2) Analyze possible outcomes (theoretical probability)

- Understand that experimental probabilities are better estimates of theoretical probabilities when they are based on larger numbers of trials

- Develop strategies for finding both experimental and theoretical probabilities

- Interpret statements of probability to make decisions and answer questions

As you work on the problems of this unit, make it a habit to ask questions about situations that involve probability and uncertainty:

What are the possible outcomes that can occur for the event in this situation?

How can I determine the experimental probability of each of the outcomes?

Is it possible to determine the theoretical probability of each of the outcomes? If so, what are these probabilities?

How can I use the probabilities to answer questions or make decisions about this situation?

A First Look at Chance

Decisions, decisions, decisions! You make decisions every day. You choose what to wear, with whom to have lunch, what to do after school, and maybe what time to go to bed.

You make some decisions without even thinking. For example, you may automatically eat the same breakfast cereal each morning. You base other decisions on how you feel at a given time. If you are in the mood to laugh, you might decide to meet a friend with a good sense of humor.

To make some decisions, you consider the chance, or likelihood, that something will happen. You may listen to the weather forecast to decide whether you will wear a raincoat to school. In some cases, you may even let chance make a decision for you, such as when you roll a number cube to see who goes first in a game.

A number cube shows the numbers 1, 2, 3, 4, 5, and 6 on its faces.

1.1 Choosing Cereal

- What are the chances of getting a 2 when you roll a number cube? Are you more likely to roll a 2 or a 6? How can you decide?

- The weather forecaster says the chance of rain tomorrow is 40%. What does this mean? Should you wear a raincoat?

- When you toss a coin, what are the chances of getting tails? If you toss seven tails in a row, are you more likely to get heads or tails on the next toss?

Kalvin always has cereal for breakfast. He likes Cocoa Blast cereal so much that he wants it every morning. Kalvin's mother wants him to eat Health Nut Flakes at least some mornings because it is more nutritious than Cocoa Blast.

Kalvin and his mother have found a fun way to choose which cereal he will have for breakfast. Each morning in June, Kalvin tosses a coin. If the coin lands on heads, he will have Cocoa Blast. If the coin lands on tails, he will have Health Nut Flakes.

Predict how many days in June Kalvin will eat Cocoa Blast.

Problem 1.1 Finding Probabilities With a Coin

A. 1. Conduct an experiment to test your prediction. Toss a coin 30 times (one for each day in June). Record your results in a table such as the one shown with 30 rows:

Coin Toss Results

Day	Result of Toss (H or T)	Number of Heads So Far	Fraction of Heads So Far	Percent of Heads So Far
1	▪	▪	▪	▪
2	▪	▪	▪	▪

2. As you add more data, what happens to the percent of tosses that are heads?

B. Work with your teacher and your classmates to combine the results from all the groups.

    1. What percent of the total number of tosses for your class is heads?

    2. As your class adds more data, what happens to the percent of tosses that are heads?

    3. Based on what you found for June, how many times do you expect Kalvin to eat Cocoa Blast in July? Explain your reasoning.

C. Kalvin's mother tells him that the chance of a coin showing heads when he tosses it is $\frac{1}{2}$. Does this mean that every time he tosses a coin twice he will get one head and one tail? Explain.

 ACE Homework starts on page 13.

1.2 Tossing Paper Cups

Kalvin really loves Cocoa Blast. He wants to find something else to toss that will give him a better chance of eating the cereal each morning. He looks through a cupboard and finds a package of paper cups. He wonders if a paper cup is a good thing to toss.

Because Kalvin wants to eat Cocoa Blast cereal more of the time, he needs to determine if the cup lands in one position more often than another. If so, he will ask to toss a paper cup instead of a coin.

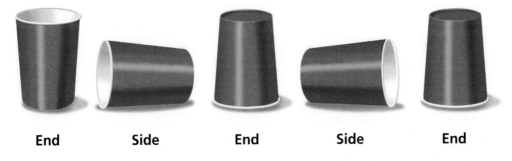

    End   **Side**   **End**   **Side**   **End**

Which of the landing positions, end or side, should Kalvin use to represent Cocoa Blast? (Remember, he wants to eat Cocoa Blast as often as possible.)

Problem (1.2) Finding More Probabilities

A. Conduct an experiment to test your prediction about how a paper cup lands. Toss a paper cup 50 times. Make a table to record your data.

B. Use your results to answer the following questions:

   1. For what fraction of your 50 tosses did the cup land on one of its ends? What percent is this?

   2. For what fraction of your 50 tosses did the cup land on its side? What percent is this?

   3. Do the landing positions *end* and *side* have the same chance of occurring? If not, which is more likely? Explain.

   4. Which of the cup's landing positions should Kalvin use to represent Cocoa Blast? Explain your reasoning.

C. Combine the data from all the groups in your class. Based on these data, would you change your answers to Question B, parts (3) and (4), above? Explain.

D. Kalvin's mom agrees to let him use a cup to decide his cereal each morning. On the first morning, the cup lands on its end. On the second morning, it lands on its side. Kalvin says, "This cup isn't any better than the coin. It lands on an end 50% of the time!" Do you agree or disagree with Kalvin? Explain.

ACE Homework starts on page 13.

1.3 One More Try

In the last two problems, you conducted experiments and found the chances of particular results. You represented these chances as fractions or percents. The mathematical word for chance is **probability**. A probability that you find by conducting an experiment and collecting data is called an **experimental probability**.

Suppose you toss a paper cup 50 times, and it lands on its side 31 times. Based on these data, the experimental probability that the cup will land on its side is $\frac{31}{50}$. Each toss of the cup is called a *trial*.

Use the ratio below to find experimental probability.

$$\frac{\text{number of favorable trials}}{\text{total number of trials}}$$

Favorable trials are the trials in which the desired result occurs. To find the probability of a cup landing on its side, count each time the cup lands on its side as a favorable trial.

You can write "the probability of the cup landing on its side" as $P(\text{side})$. In the experiment just described,

$$P(\text{side}) = \frac{\text{number of times cup landed on its side}}{\text{number of times cup was tossed}} = \frac{31}{50}.$$

Kalvin has come up with one more way to use probability to decide his breakfast cereal. This time, he tosses two coins.

- If the coins match, he gets to eat Cocoa Blast.

Match

Match

- If the coins do not match, he eats Health Nut Flakes.

No Match

Suppose his mother agrees to let him use this method. How many days in June do you think Kalvin will eat Cocoa Blast?

Problem 1.3 Finding Experimental Probabilities

A. 1. Conduct an experiment by tossing a pair of coins 30 times. Keep track of the number of times the coins *match* and the number of times a *no-match* occurs.

   2. Based on your data, what is the experimental probability of getting a match? Of getting a no-match?

B. Combine your data with your classmates' data.

   1. Find the experimental probabilities for the combined data. Compare these probabilities with the probabilities in Question A.

   2. Based on the class data, do you think a match and a no-match have the same chance of occurring? Explain.

C. Think about the possible results when you toss two coins.

   1. In how many ways can a match occur?

   2. In how many ways can a no-match occur?

   3. Based on the number of ways each result can occur, do a match and a no-match have the same chance of occurring? Explain.

D. Kalvin's friend Asta suggests that he toss a thumbtack. If it lands on its side, he eats Cocoa Blast. If it lands on its head, he eats Health Nut Flakes. She says they must first experiment to find the probabilities involved. Asta does 11 tosses. Kalvin does 50 tosses. Here are the probabilities they find based on their experiments:

   Asta: $P(\text{heads}) = \dfrac{6}{11}$ Kalvin: $P(\text{heads}) = \dfrac{13}{50}$

   Which result do you think better predicts the thumbtack landing on its head when tossed? Explain.

ACE Homework starts on page 13.

Kalvin finds a coin near a railroad track. It looks flat and a little bent, so he guesses it has been run over by a train. He decides to use this unusual coin to choose his breakfast cereal during November. By the end of the month, he has had Health Nut Flakes only seven times. His mother is suspicious of the coin. She wonders if the coin is fair.

- Why do you think Kalvin's mother is suspicious of the coin?
- What do you think it means for a coin to be "fair"?

Kalvin's mother explains why she is suspicious. "With a fair coin, heads and tails are **equally likely.** This means that you have the same chance of getting heads as tails." Kalvin is not sure what his mother means by "equally likely," so she uses an example to help explain.

"Suppose each person in our family writes his or her name on a card and puts the card in a hat. If you mix up the cards and pull one out, each name is equally likely to be picked. But suppose I put my name in the hat ten times. Then, the names are not equally likely to be picked. My name has a greater chance of being chosen."

Problem 1.4 Understanding Equally Likely Events

A. The table below lists several actions and possible results. In each case, decide whether the possible results are equally likely and explain. For actions 5–7, start by listing all the possible results.

Action	**Possible Results**
1. You toss an empty juice can.	The can lands on its side, the can lands upside down, or the can lands right side up.
2. A baby is born.	The baby is a boy or the baby is a girl.

Action	**Possible Results**
3. A baby is born.	The baby is right-handed or the baby is left-handed.
4. The Pittsburgh Steelers play a football game.	The Steelers win, the Steelers lose, or the Steelers tie.
5. You roll a six-sided number cube.	_____
6. You guess an answer on a true/false test.	_____
7. In basketball, you attempt a free throw.	_____

B. For which of the actions in Question A did you find the results to be equally likely? Does this mean that the probability of each result is $\frac{1}{2}$ (or 50%)? Explain.

C. Describe an action for which the results are equally likely. Then, describe an action for which the results are *not* equally likely.

ACE Homework starts on page 13.

Applications

1. a. Miki tosses a coin 50 times and the coin shows heads 28 times. What fraction of the 50 tosses is heads? What percent is this?

   b. Suppose the coin is fair, and Miki tosses it 500 times. About how many times can she expect it to show heads? Explain your reasoning.

For: Multiple-Choice Skills Practice
Web Code: ama-7154

2. Suppose Kalvin tosses a coin to determine his breakfast cereal every day. He starts on his twelfth birthday and continues until his eighteenth birthday. About how many times would you expect him to eat Cocoa Blast cereal?

3. Kalvin tosses a coin five days in a row and gets tails every time. Do you think there is something wrong with the coin? How can you find out?

4. Len tosses a coin three times. The coin shows heads every time. What are the chances the coin shows tails on the next toss? Explain.

5. Is it possible to toss a coin 20 times and have it land heads up 20 times? Is this likely to happen? Explain.

6. Kalvin tosses a paper cup once each day for a year to determine his breakfast cereal. Use your results from Problem 1.2 to answer the following.

   a. How many times do you expect the cup to land on its side? On one of its ends?

   b. How many times a month do you expect Kalvin to eat Cocoa Blast? How many times a year? Explain.

7. Dawn tosses a pawn from her chess set five times. It lands on its base four times and on its side only once.

Andre tosses the same pawn 100 times. It lands on its base 28 times and on its side 72 times. Based on their data, if you toss the pawn one more time, is it more likely to land on its base or its side? Why?

8. Kalvin flips a small paper cup 50 times and a large paper cup 30 times. The table below displays the results of his experiments. Based on this data, should he use the small cup or the large cup to determine his breakfast each morning? Explain.

Homework Help Online PHSchool.com

For: Help with Exercise 8
Web Code: ame-7108

Paper Cup Toss Results

Where Cup Lands	Small Paper Cup	Large Paper Cup
Side	39 times	22 times
One of Its Ends	11 times	8 times

9. Kalvin's sister Kyla finds yet another way for him to pick his breakfast. She places one blue marble and one red marble in each of two bags. She says that each morning he can choose one marble from each bag. If the marbles are the same color, he eats Cocoa Blast. If not, he eats Health Nut Flakes. Explain how selecting one marble from each of the two bags and tossing two coins are similar.

10. Brooke and Jake have to decide who will take out the garbage. Jake suggests they toss two coins. If at least one head comes up, Brooke takes out the garbage. If no heads come up, Jake takes out the garbage. Should Brooke agree to Jake's proposal? Why or why not?

For Exercises 11–15, decide whether the possible results are equally likely. Explain.

Action	Possible Results
11. Your phone rings at 9:00 P.M.	The caller is your best friend, the caller is a relative, or the caller is someone else.
12. You check the temperature in your area tomorrow morning.	The temperature is 30°F or higher, or the temperature is below 30°F.
13. You spin the pointer once. 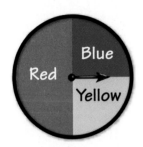	The pointer lands on yellow, the pointer lands on red, or the pointer lands on blue.
14. You find out how many car accidents occurred in your city or town yesterday.	There were fewer than five accidents, there were exactly five accidents, or there were more than five accidents.
15. You choose a card from a standard deck of playing cards (with no jokers).	The card is a spade, the card is a heart, the card is a diamond, or the card is a club.

For Exercises 16 and 17, first list all the possible results for each action. Then, decide whether the results are equally likely.

16. You choose a block from a bag containing one red block, three blue blocks, and one green block.

17. You try to steal second base during a baseball game.

18. For parts (a)–(f), give an example of a result that would have a probability near the percent given.

   a. 0%   **b.** 25%   **c.** 50%

   d. 75%   **e.** 80%   **f.** 100%

Connections

19. Colby rolls a number cube several times. She records the result of each roll and organizes her data in the table below.

Number Cube Results

Number	Times the Number is Rolled
1							
2										
3							
4									
5												
6											

   a. What fraction of the rolls are 2's? What percent is this?

   b. What fraction of the rolls are odd numbers? What percent is this?

   c. What percent of the rolls is greater than 3?

   d. Suppose Colby rolls the number cube 100 times. About how many times can she expect to roll a 2? Explain.

   e. If Colby rolls the number cube 1,000 times, about how many times can she expect to roll an odd number? Explain.

20. For each pair of fractions, find a fraction between the two fractions.

   a. $\frac{1}{10}$ and $\frac{8}{25}$ **b.** $\frac{3}{8}$ and $\frac{11}{40}$

For Exercises 21–23, use the bar graph below.

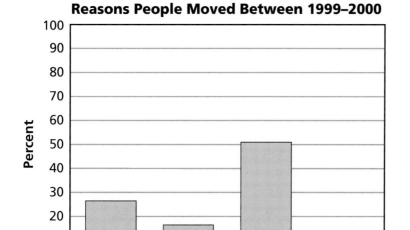

Reasons People Moved Between 1999–2000

SOURCE: U.S. Census Bureau

21. Multiple Choice Suppose 41,642 people moved. About how many of these people moved for family-related reasons?

   A. 28   **B.** 11,000   **C.** 21,000   **D.** 31,000

22. Multiple Choice About what fraction of the people represented in the chart moved for reasons other than work-related, housing-related, or family-related?

   F. $\frac{6}{10}$ **G.** $\frac{6}{100}$ **H.** $\frac{52}{100}$ **J.** $\frac{94}{100}$

23. Multiple Choice Suppose 41,642 people moved. About how many of these people moved for housing-related reasons?

   A. 52   **B.** 11,000   **C.** 21,000   **D.** 31,000

24. Suppose you write each factor of 42 on pieces of paper and put them in a bag. You shake the bag and then choose one piece of paper from the bag. Find the probability of choosing a factor that is

   a. an even number.

   b. a prime number.

25. Weather forecasters often use percents to give probabilities in their forecasts. For example, a forecaster might say that there is a 50% chance of rain tomorrow. For the forecasts below, change the fractional probabilities to percents.

   a. The probability that it will rain tomorrow is $\frac{2}{5}$.

   b. The probability that it will snow Monday is $\frac{3}{10}$.

   c. The probability that it will be cloudy this weekend is $\frac{3}{5}$.

26. Waldo, the meteorologist from WARM radio, boasts that he is the best weather predictor in Sunspot, South Carolina. On Monday, Waldo says, "There is only a 10% chance of rain tomorrow!"

   a. Ask at least two adults what they think Waldo's statement means. Write down their explanations.

   b. Explain what you think Waldo's statement means.

   c. If it rains on Tuesday, is Waldo wrong? Why or why not?

For Exercises 27–30, use this graph, which shows the average number of tornadoes per year in several states.

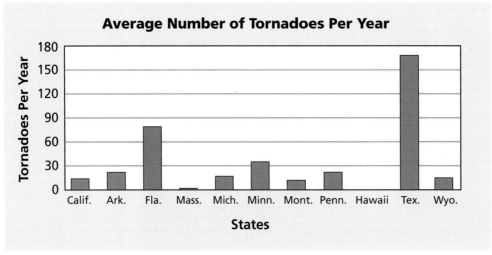

Source: National Oceanic and Atmospheric Administration

27. In an average year, is a tornado equally likely to occur in California as in Florida? Explain your reasoning.

28. In an average year, is a tornado equally likely to occur in Arkansas as in Pennsylvania?

29. In an average year, is a tornado equally likely to occur in Massachusetts as in Texas?

30. Based on these data, is a person living in Montana more likely to experience a tornado than a person living in Massachusetts? Explain.

Extensions

31. Monday is the first day Kalvin tosses a coin to determine his cereal. During the first five days, he has Cocoa Blast only twice. One possible pattern of Kalvin's coin tosses is shown.

Coin Toss Results

Monday	Tuesday	Wednesday	Thursday	Friday
H	H	T	T	T

Find every way Kalvin can toss the coin during the week and have Cocoa Blast cereal twice. Explain how you know that you found every possible way.

32. Yolanda watches a carnival game in which a paper cup is tossed. It costs $1 to play the game. If the cup lands upright, the player wins $5. The cup is tossed 50 times. It lands on its side 32 times, upside down 13 times, and upright 5 times.

a. If Yolanda plays the game ten times, about how many times can she expect to win? How many times can she expect to lose?

b. Do you expect her to have more or less money at the end of ten games? Why?

Mathematical Reflections 1

In this investigation, you conducted experiments with coins and paper cups. You used fractions and percents to express the chances, or probabilities, that certain results would occur. You also considered several actions and determined whether the possible results were equally likely. These questions will help you summarize what you have learned.

Think about your answers to these questions. Discuss your ideas with other students and your teacher. Then write a summary of your findings in your notebook.

1. How do you find the experimental probability that a particular result will occur? Why is it called the experimental probability?

2. In an experiment, are 30 trials as good as 500 trials to predict the chances of a result? Explain.

3. What does it mean for results to be equally likely?

Investigation 2

Experimental and Theoretical Probability

In the last investigation, you collected the results of many coin tosses. You found that the experimental probability of a coin landing on heads is $\frac{1}{2}$ (or very close to $\frac{1}{2}$).

The results of the coin-tossing experiment probably didn't surprise you. You already knew that the two possible results, heads and tails, are equally likely. In fact, you can find the probability of tossing heads by examining the possible results rather than by experimenting. There are two equally likely results. Because one of the results is heads, the probability of tossing heads is 1 of 2, or $\frac{1}{2}$.

The individual results of an action or event are called **outcomes.** The coin-tossing experiment had two outcomes, heads and tails. A probability calculated by examining outcomes, rather than by experimenting, is a **theoretical probability.**

When the outcomes of an action or event are equally likely, you can use the ratio below to find the theoretical probability.

$$\frac{\text{number of favorable outcomes}}{\text{number of possible outcomes}}$$

Favorable outcomes are the outcomes in which you are interested.

You can write the theoretical probability of tossing heads as $P(\text{heads})$. So,

$$P(\text{heads}) = \frac{\text{number of ways heads can occur}}{\text{number of outcomes}} = \frac{1}{2}.$$

In this investigation, you will explore some other situations in which probabilities are found both by experimenting and by analyzing the possible outcomes.

Predicting to Win

In the last 5 minutes of the *Gee Whiz Everyone Wins!* game show, all the members of the audience are called to the stage. They each choose a block at *random* from a bucket containing an unknown number of red, yellow, and blue blocks. Each block has the same size and shape. Before choosing, each contestant predicts the color of his or her block. If the prediction is correct, the contestant wins. After each selection, the block is put back into the bucket.

What do you think random *means? Suppose you are a member of the audience. Would you rather be called to the stage first or last? Why?*

Problem 2.1 Finding Theoretical Probabilities

A. 1. Play the block-guessing game with your class. Keep a record of the number of times a color is chosen. Play the game until you think you can predict the chances of each color being chosen.

　2. Based on the data you collect during the game, find the experimental probabilities of choosing red, choosing yellow, and choosing blue.

B. 1. After you look in the bucket, find the fraction of the blocks that are red, the fraction that are yellow, and the fraction that are blue. These are the theoretical probabilities.

　2. How do the theoretical probabilities compare to the experimental probabilities in Question A?

　3. What is the sum of the theoretical probabilities in Question B, part (1)?

C. 1. Does each block have an equally likely chance of being chosen? Explain.

　2. Does each color have an equally likely chance of being chosen? Explain.

D. Which person has the advantage—the first person to choose from the bucket or the last person? Explain.

`ACE` **Homework starts on page 28.**

2.2 Exploring Probabilities

In the next problem set, you will discover some interesting facts about probabilities.

Problem 2.2 Exploring Probabilities

A. A bag contains two yellow marbles, four blue marbles, and six red marbles. You choose a marble from the bag at random.

    1. What is the probability the marble is yellow? The probability it is blue? The probability it is red?

    2. What is the sum of the probabilities from part (1)?

    3. What color is the marble most likely to be?

    4. What is the probability the marble is *not* blue?

    5. What is the probability the marble is either red or yellow?

    6. What is the probability the marble is white?

    7. Mary says the probability the marble is blue is $\frac{12}{4}$. Anne says $\frac{12}{4}$ is impossible. Who is correct? Explain your reasoning.

B. Suppose the bag in Question A has twice as many marbles of each color. Do the probabilities change? Explain.

C. How many blue marbles do you add to the bag in Question A to have the probability of choosing a blue marble equal to $\frac{1}{2}$?

D. A bag contains several marbles. Each marble is either red, white, or blue. The probability of choosing a red marble is $\frac{1}{3}$, and the probability of choosing a white marble is $\frac{1}{6}$.

    1. What is the probability of choosing a blue marble? Explain.

    2. What is the least number of marbles that can be in the bag? Explain. Suppose the bag contains the least number of marbles. How many of each color does the bag contain?

    3. Can the bag contain 48 marbles? If so, how many of each color would it contain?

    4. Suppose the bag contains 8 red marbles and 4 white marbles. How many blue marbles does it contain?

ACE Homework starts on page 28.

To find the theoretical probability of a result, you need to count all the possible outcomes. In some situations, such as when you toss a coin or roll a number cube, it is easy to count the outcomes. In other situations, it can be difficult. One way to find (or count) all the possible outcomes is to make an organized list. Here is an organized list of all the possible outcomes of tossing two coins.

First Coin	Second Coin	Outcome
heads	heads	heads-heads
heads	tails	heads-tails
tails	heads	tails-heads
tails	tails	tails-tails

Another way to find all possible outcomes is to make a **tree diagram.** A tree diagram is a diagram that shows all the possible outcomes of an event. The steps for making a counting tree for tossing two coins are shown below.

Step 1 Label a starting point. Make a branch from the starting point for each possible result for the first coin.

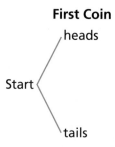

Step 2 Make a branch from each of the results for the first coin to show the possible results for the second coin.

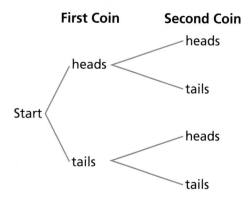

Step 3 When you follow the paths from left to right, you can find all the possible outcomes of tossing two coins. For example, the path shown in red represents the outcome heads-heads.

First Coin	Second Coin	Outcome
heads	heads	heads-heads
	tails	heads-tails
tails	heads	tails-heads
	tails	tails-tails

Both the organized list and the tree diagram show that there are four possible outcomes when you toss two coins. The outcomes are equally likely, so the probability of each outcome is $\frac{1}{4}$.

$$P(\text{heads, heads}) = \frac{1}{4}$$
$$P(\text{heads, tails}) = \frac{1}{4}$$
$$P(\text{tails, heads}) = \frac{1}{4}$$
$$P(\text{tails, tails}) = \frac{1}{4}$$

If you toss two coins, what is the probability that the coins will match?

What is the probability they won't match?

All the winners from the *Gee Whiz Everyone Wins!* game show have the opportunity to compete for a bonus prize. Each winner chooses one block from each of two bags. Both bags contain one red, one yellow, and one blue block. The contestant must predict which color she or he will choose from each of the two bags. If the prediction is correct, the contestant wins a $10,000 bonus prize!

What are the contestant's chances of winning this game?

Problem 2.3 Using Strategies to Find Theoretical Probabilities

A. 1. Conduct an experiment with 36 trials for the situation above. Record the pairs of colors that you choose.

2. Find the experimental probability of choosing each possible pair of colors.

3. If you combined your data with the data collected by your classmates, would your answer to part (1) change? Explain.

B. 1. List all the possible pairs that can be chosen. Are these outcomes equally likely? Explain your reasoning.

2. Find the theoretical probability of choosing each pair of blocks.

3. Does a contestant have a chance to win the bonus prize? Is it likely a contestant will win the bonus prize? Explain.

4. If you play this game 18 times, about how many times do you expect to win?

C. How do the theoretical probabilities compare with your experimental probabilities? Explain any differences.

ACE **Homework starts on page 28.**

2.4 Pondering Possible and Probable

Santo and Tevy are playing a coin-tossing game. To play the game, they take turns tossing three coins. If all three coins match, Santo wins. Otherwise, Tevy wins. Both players have won the game several times, but Tevy seems to be winning more often. Santo thinks the game is unfair.

Do you think this game is fair?

Problem 2.4 Pondering Possible and Probable

A. 1. How many possible outcomes are there when you toss three coins? Show all your work. Are the outcomes equally likely?

   2. What is the theoretical probability that the three coins will match?

   3. What is the theoretical probability that exactly two coins will match?

   4. Is this a fair game? Explain your reasoning.

B. If you tossed three coins 24 times, how many times would you expect two coins to match?

C. Santo said, "It is *possible* to toss three matching coins." Tevy replied, "Yes, but is it *probable*?" What do you think each boy meant?

ACE Homework starts on page 28.

Applications

1. A bucket contains one green block, one red block, and two yellow blocks. You choose one block from the bucket.

   a. Find the theoretical probability that you will choose each color.

   $P(\text{green}) = \blacksquare$ $P(\text{yellow}) = \blacksquare$ $P(\text{red}) = \blacksquare$

   b. Find the sum of the probabilities in part (a).

   c. What is the probability that you will *not* choose a red block? Explain how you found your answer.

   d. What is the sum of the probability of choosing a red block and the probability of *not* choosing a red block?

2. A bubble-gum machine contains 25 gumballs. There are 12 green, 6 purple, 2 orange, and 5 yellow gumballs.

   a. Find each theoretical probability.

   $P(\text{green}) = \blacksquare$ $P(\text{purple}) = \blacksquare$

   $P(\text{orange}) = \blacksquare$ $P(\text{yellow}) = \blacksquare$

   b. Find the sum.

   $P(\text{green}) + P(\text{purple}) + P(\text{orange}) + P(\text{yellow}) = \blacksquare$

   c. Write each of the probabilities in part (a) as a percent.

   $P(\text{green}) = \blacksquare$ $P(\text{purple}) = \blacksquare$

   $P(\text{orange}) = \blacksquare$ $P(\text{yellow}) = \blacksquare$

   d. What is the sum of all the probabilities as a percent?

   e. What do you think the sum of the probabilities for all the possible outcomes must be for any situation? Explain.

3. A bag contains two white blocks, one red block, and three purple blocks. You choose one block from the bag.

  a. Find each probability.

  $P(\text{white}) = $ $P(\text{red}) = $  $P(\text{purple}) = $

  b. What is the probability of *not* choosing a white block? Explain how you found your answer.

  c. Suppose the number of blocks of each color is doubled. What happens to the probability of choosing each color?

  d. Suppose you add two more blocks of each color. What happens to the probability of choosing each color?

  e. How many blocks of which colors should you add to the original bag to make the probability of choosing a red block equal to $\frac{1}{2}$?

4. A bag contains exactly three blue blocks. You choose a block at random. Find each probability.

  a. $P(\text{blue})$ **b.** $P(not \text{ blue})$ **c.** $P(\text{yellow})$

Go Online
PHSchool.com

For: Multiple-Choice Skills Practice
Web Code: ama-7254

5. A bag contains several marbles. Some are red, some are white, and some are blue. You count the marbles and find the theoretical probability of choosing a red marble is $\frac{1}{5}$. You also find the theoretical probability of choosing a white marble is $\frac{3}{10}$.

  a. What is the least number of marbles that can be in the bag?

  b. Can the bag contain 60 marbles? If so, how many of each color does it contain?

  c. If the bag contains 4 red marbles and 6 white marbles, how many blue marbles does it contain?

  d. How can you find the probability of choosing a blue marble?

6. Decide whether each statement is true or false. Justify your answers.

  a. The probability of an outcome can be 0.

  b. The probability of an outcome can be 1.

  c. The probability of an outcome can be greater than 1.

7. Melissa is designing a birthday card for her sister. She has a blue, a yellow, a pink, and a green sheet of paper. She also has a black, a red, and a purple marker. Suppose Melissa chooses one sheet of paper and one marker at random.

   a. Make a tree diagram to find all the possible color combinations.

   b. What is the probability that Melissa chooses pink paper and a red marker?

   c. What is the probability that Melissa chooses blue paper? What is the probability she does *not* choose blue paper?

   d. What is the probability that she chooses a purple marker?

8. Lunch at Casimer Middle School consists of a sandwich, a vegetable, and a fruit. Today there is an equal number of each type of sandwich, vegetable, and fruit. The students don't know what lunch they will get. Sol's favorite lunch is a chicken sandwich, carrots, and a banana.

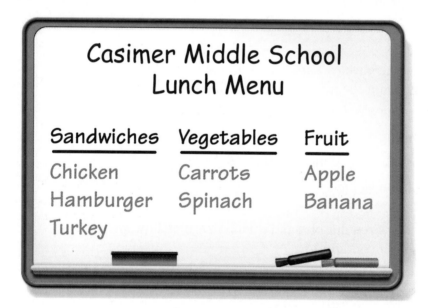

Casimer Middle School Lunch Menu

Sandwiches	Vegetables	Fruit
Chicken	Carrots	Apple
Hamburger	Spinach	Banana
Turkey		

   a. Make a tree diagram to determine how many different lunches are possible. List all the possible outcomes.

   b. What is the probability that Sol gets his favorite lunch? Explain your reasoning.

   c. What is the probability that Sol gets at least one of his favorite lunch items? Explain.

9. Suppose you spin the pointer of the spinner at the right once and roll the number cube. (The numbers on the cube are 1, 2, 3, 4, 5, and 6.)

   a. Make a tree diagram of the possible outcomes of a spin of the pointer and a roll of the number cube.

   b. What is the probability that you get a 2 on both the spinner and the number cube? Explain your reasoning.

   c. What is the probability that you get a factor of 2 on both the spinner and the number cube?

   d. What is the probability that you get a multiple of 2 on both the number cube and the spinner?

10. Patricia and Jean design a coin-tossing game. Patricia suggests tossing three coins. Jean says they can toss one coin three times. Are the outcomes different for the two situations? Explain.

11. Pietro and Eva are playing a game in which they toss a coin three times. Eva gets a point if *no* two consecutive toss results match (as in H-T-H). Pietro gets a point if exactly two consecutive toss results match (as in H-H-T). The first player to get 10 points wins. Is this a fair game? Explain. If it is not a fair game, change the rules to make it fair.

12. Silvia and Juanita are designing a game. In the game, you toss two number cubes and consider whether the sum of the two numbers is odd or even. They make a tree diagram of possible outcomes.

Homework Help Online PHSchool.com

For: Help with Exercise 12
Web Code: ame-7212

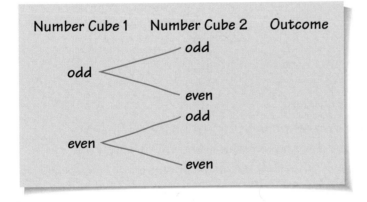

   a. List all the outcomes.

   b. Design rules for a two-player game that is fair.

   c. Design rules for a two-player game that is not fair.

   d. How is this situation similar to tossing two coins and seeing if the coins match or don't match?

Connections

13. Find numbers that make each sentence true.

    a. $\dfrac{1}{8} = \dfrac{\blacksquare}{32} = \dfrac{5}{\blacksquare}$ **b.** $\dfrac{3}{7} = \dfrac{\blacksquare}{21} = \dfrac{6}{\blacksquare}$ **c.** $\dfrac{6}{20} = \dfrac{\blacksquare}{5} = \dfrac{12}{\blacksquare}$

14. Which of the following sums is equal to 1?

    a. $\dfrac{1}{6} + \dfrac{3}{6} + \dfrac{2}{6}$ **b.** $\dfrac{4}{18} + \dfrac{1}{9} + \dfrac{2}{3}$ **c.** $\dfrac{1}{5} + \dfrac{1}{3} + \dfrac{1}{5}$

15. From Question 14, choose a sum equal to 1. Describe a situation whose events have a theoretical probability that can be represented by the sum.

16. Kara and Bly both perform the same experiment in math class. Kara gets a probability of $\dfrac{125}{300}$ and Bly gets a probability of $\dfrac{108}{320}$.

    a. Whose experimental probability is closer to the theoretical probability of $\dfrac{1}{3}$? Explain your reasoning.

    b. Give two possible experiments that Kara and Bly can do that have a theoretical probability of $\dfrac{1}{3}$.

For Exercises 17–24, estimate the probability that the given event occurs. Any probability must be between 0 and 1 (or 0% and 100%). If an event is impossible, the probability it will occur is 0, or 0%. If an event is certain to happen, the probability it will occur is 1, or 100%.

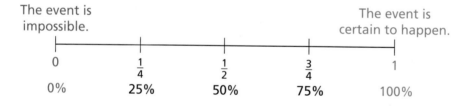

Sample   You watch television tonight.

         I watch some television every night, unless I have too much homework. So far, I do not have much homework today. I am about 95% sure that I will watch television tonight.

17. You are absent from school at least one day during this school year.

18. You have pizza for lunch one day this week.

19. It snows on July 4 this year in Mexico.

20. You get all the problems on your next math test correct.

21. The next baby born in your local hospital is a girl.

22. The sun sets tonight.

23. You win a game by tossing four coins. The result is all heads.

24. You toss a coin and get 100 tails in a row.

Multiple Choice For Exercises 25–28, choose the fraction closest to the given decimal.

25. 0.39

A. $\frac{1}{2}$ **B.** $\frac{1}{4}$ **C.** $\frac{1}{8}$ **D.** $\frac{1}{10}$

26. 0.125

F. $\frac{1}{2}$ **G.** $\frac{1}{4}$ **H.** $\frac{1}{8}$ **J.** $\frac{1}{10}$

27. 0.195

A. $\frac{1}{2}$ **B.** $\frac{1}{4}$ **C.** $\frac{1}{8}$ **D.** $\frac{1}{10}$

28. 0.24

F. $\frac{1}{2}$ **G.** $\frac{1}{4}$ **H.** $\frac{1}{8}$ **J.** $\frac{1}{10}$

29. Koto's class makes the line plot shown below. Each mark represents the first letter of the name of a student in her class.

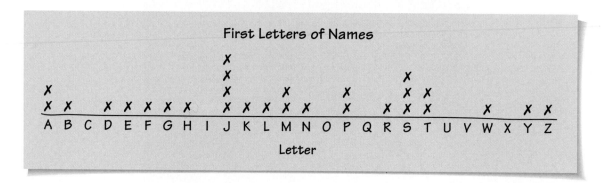

First Letters of Names

Letter

Suppose you choose a student at random from Koto's Class.

a. What is the probability that the student's name begins with J?

b. What is the probability that the student's name begins with a letter after F and before T in the alphabet?

c. What is the probability that you choose Koto?

d. Suppose two new students, Melvin and Tara, join the class. You now choose a student at random from the class. What is the probability that the student's name begins with J?

30. A bag contains red, white, blue, and green marbles. The probability of choosing a red marble is $\frac{1}{7}$. The probability of choosing a green marble is $\frac{1}{2}$. The probability of choosing a white marble is half the probability of choosing a red one. You want to find the number of marbles in the bag.

a. Why do you need to know how to multiply and add fractions to proceed?

b. Why do you need to know about multiples of whole numbers to proceed?

c. Can there be seven marbles in the bag? Explain.

31. Write the following as one fraction.

a. $\frac{1}{2}$ of $\frac{1}{7}$

b. $\frac{1}{7} + \frac{1}{14} + \frac{1}{2}$

32. Karen and Mia play games with coins and number cubes. No matter which game they play, Karen loses more often than Mia. Karen is not sure if she just has bad luck or if the games are unfair. The games are described in this table. Review the game rules and complete the table.

Games	Is It Possible for Karen to Win?	Is It Likely Karen Will Win?	Is the Game Fair or Unfair?
Game 1 Roll a number cube. • Karen scores a point if the roll is even. • Mia scores a point if the roll is odd.			
Game 2 Roll a number cube. • Karen scores a point if the roll is a multiple of 4. • Mia scores a point if the roll is a multiple of 3.			
Game 3 Toss two coins. • Karen scores a point if the coins match. • Mia scores a point if the coins do not match.			
Game 4 Roll two number cubes. • Karen scores a point if the number cubes match. • Mia scores a point if the number cubes do not match.			
Game 5 Roll two number cubes. • Karen scores a point if the product of the two numbers is 7. • Mia scores a point if the sum of the two numbers is 7.			

33. Karen and Mia invent another game. They roll a number cube twice and read the two digits shown as a two-digit number. So if Karen gets a 6 and then a 2, she has 62.

    a. What is the least number possible?

    b. What is the greatest number possible?

    c. Are all numbers equally likely?

    d. Suppose Karen wins on any prime number and Mia wins on any multiple of 4. Explain how to decide who is more likely to win.

Extensions

34. Place 12 objects of the same size and shape in a bag such as blocks or marbles. Use three or four different solid colors.

    a. Describe the contents of your bag.

    b. Determine the theoretical probability of choosing each color by examining the bag's contents.

    c. Conduct an experiment to determine the experimental probability of choosing each color. Describe your experiment and record your results.

    d. How do the two types of probability compare?

35. Suppose you are a contestant on the *Gee Whiz Everyone Wins!* game show in Problem 2.3. You win a mountain bike, a CD player, a vacation to Hawaii, and a one-year membership to an amusement park. You play the bonus round and lose. Then the host makes this offer:

> You can choose from the two bags again. If the two colors match, you win $5,000. If the two colors do not match, you do not get the $5,000 and you return all the prizes.

Would you accept this offer? Explain.

36. Suppose you compete for the bonus prize on the *Gee Whiz Everyone Wins!* game in Problem 2.3. You choose one block from each of two bags. Each bag contains one red, one yellow, and one blue block.

   a. Make a tree diagram to show all the possible outcomes.

   b. What is the probability that you choose two blocks that are *not* blue?

   c. Jason made the tree diagram shown below to find the probability of choosing two blocks that are *not* blue. Using his tree, what probability do you think Jason got?

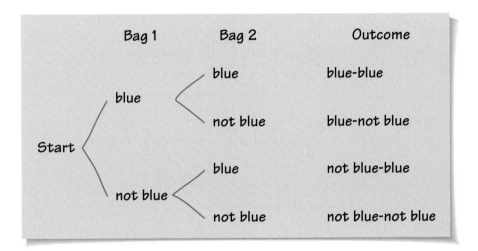

   d. Does your answer in part (b) match Jason's? If not, why do you think Jason gets a different answer?

37. Suppose you toss four coins.

   a. List all the possible outcomes.

   b. What is the probability of each outcome?

   c. Design a game for two players that involves tossing four coins. What is the probability that each player wins? Is one player more likely to win than the other player?

Connections Extensions

Mathematical Reflections 2

In this investigation, you explored two ways to get information about the probability that something will occur. You can design an experiment and collect data (to find experimental probabilities), or you can think about a situation and analyze it carefully to see exactly what might happen (to find theoretical probabilities). These questions will help you summarize what you have learned.

Think about your answers to these questions. Discuss your ideas with other students and your teacher. Then write a summary of your findings in your notebook.

1. Describe how you can find the theoretical probability of an outcome. Why is it called a theoretical probability?

2. **a.** Suppose two people do an experiment to estimate the probability that an outcome occurs. Will they get the same probabilities? Explain.

   b. Suppose two people analyze a situation to find the theoretical probability that an outcome occurs. Will they get the same probabilities? Explain.

   c. One person uses an experiment to estimate the probability that an outcome occurs. Another person analyzes the situation to find the theoretical probability that the outcome can occur. Will they get the same probabilities? Explain.

Investigation 3

Making Decisions With Probability

Spring vacation has arrived! Kalvin thinks he can stay up until 11:00 P.M. every night. His father thinks Kalvin will have more energy for his activities (such as roller blading, cleaning out the garage, or washing dishes) during his vacation if he goes to bed at 9:00 P.M.

3.1 Designing a Spinner

Getting Ready for Problem 3.1

Kalvin makes the three spinners shown below. Kalvin hopes that his father lets him use one of the spinners to determine his bedtime.

Spinner 1

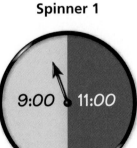

9:00   11:00

Spinner 2

9:00

11:00

Spinner 3

9:00   11:00

11:00   9:00

- Which spinner gives Kalvin the best chance of going to bed at 11:00? Explain.

Kalvin decides to design a spinner that lands on 11:00 the most. To convince his father to use this spinner, Kalvin puts three 9:00 spaces, two 10:00 spaces, and one 11:00 space on the spinner. However, he uses the biggest space for 11:00. Kalvin hopes the pointer lands on that space the most.

Which time do you think is most likely to occur?

Problem 3.1 Finding Probabilities With a Spinner

A. 1. Find the experimental probability that the pointer lands on 9:00, on 10:00, and on 11:00.

   2. After how many spins did you decide to stop spinning? Why?

   3. Suppose Kalvin spins the pointer 64 times. Based on your experiment, how many times can he expect the pointer to land on 9:00, on 10:00, and on 11:00?

B. 1. What is the theoretical probability that the pointer lands on 9:00, on 10:00, and on 11:00? Explain.

   2. Suppose Kalvin spins the pointer 64 times. Based on your theoretical probabilities, how many times can he expect the pointer to land on 9:00, on 10:00, and on 11:00?

   3. How do your answers to Question A part (3) and Question B part (2) compare?

C. Describe one way Kalvin's father can design a spinner so that Kalvin is most likely to go to bed at 9:00.

ACE Homework starts on page 44.

3.2 Making Decisions

Kalvin begins to think that probability is a good way to make decisions. One day at school, Kalvin's teacher, Ms. Miller, has to decide which student to send to the office to get an important message. Billie, Evo, and Carla volunteer. Kalvin suggests they design a quick experiment to choose the student fairly.

Getting Ready for Problem 3.2

Which of these items can Kalvin's class use to choose a messenger? How can they make the decision fair?

- a coin
- a six-sided number cube
- colored cubes
- playing cards
- a spinner

Problem **3.2** Analyzing Fairness

Two suggestions for making a decision are shown in each question. Decide whether the suggestions are fair ways to make the decision. Explain your reasoning.

A. At lunch, Kalvin and his friends discuss whether to play kickball, soccer, baseball, or dodgeball. Ethan and Ava each have a suggestion.

Ethan: We can make a spinner that looks like this:

Ava: We can roll a number cube. If it lands on 1, we play kickball. A roll of 2 means soccer, 3 means baseball, 4 means dodgeball, and we can roll again if it's 5 or 6.

B. The group decides to play baseball. Tony and Meda are the team captains. Now they must decide who bats first.

Tony: We can roll a number cube. If the number is a multiple of three, my team bats first. Otherwise, Meda's team bats first.

Meda: Yes, let's roll a number cube, but my team bats first if the number is even and Tony's team bats first if it's odd.

C. There are 60 sixth-grade students at Kalvin's school. The students need to choose someone to wear the mascot costume on field day.

Huey: We can give everyone a number from 1 to 60. Then, we can roll 10 number cubes and add the results. The person whose number is equal to the sum wears the costume.

Sal: That doesn't seem fair. Everyone should have a number from 0 to 59. In one bag, we can have blocks numbered 0 to 5. In another bag, we can have blocks numbered 0 to 9. We can select one block from the first bag to represent the tens digit and one block from the second bag to represent the ones digit.

ACE Homework starts on page 44.

3.3 Scratching Spots

Have you ever tried to win a contest? Probability can often help you figure out your chances of winning.

Tawanda's Toys is having a contest. Any customer who spends at least $10 receives a scratch-off prize card.

- Each card has five gold spots that reveal the names of video games when you scratch them.

- Exactly two spots match on each card.

- A customer may scratch off only two spots on a card.

- If the spots match, the customer wins that video game.

It can be difficult to get enough prize cards to conduct an experiment. So, you can design a related experiment to help you find the probability of each outcome. A model used to find experimental probabilities is a **simulation.**

One way you can simulate the scratch-off card is by using five playing cards. First, make sure that exactly two out of the five cards match. Place the cards facedown on a table. While your eyes are closed, have a friend mix up the cards. Then open your eyes and choose two cards. If the cards match, you win. Otherwise, you lose.

Can you think of another way to simulate the scratch-off cards?

Problem 3.3 Using a Simulation

A. Use the card simulation above to find the probability of winning.

B. Examine the different ways you can scratch off two spots. Find the theoretical probability of winning with one prize card.

C. Suppose you have 100 prize cards from Tawanda.

  1. How many video games can you expect to win?

  2. How much money do you need to get 100 cards?

D. Tawanda thinks she may lose money with this promotion. The video games she gives away cost her $15 each. Will Tawanda lose money? Why or why not?

ACE Homework starts on page 44.

Applications

1. For parts (a)–(g), use a spinner similar to the one below.

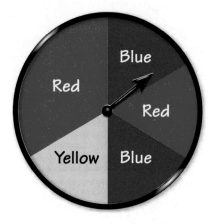

a. Use a paper clip or bobby pin as a pointer. Spin the pointer 30 times. What fraction of your spins land on red? What fraction land on blue? On yellow?

b. Use an angle ruler or another method to examine the spinner. What fraction of the spinner is red? What fraction is blue? What fraction is yellow? Explain.

c. Compare your answers to parts (a) and (b). Do you expect these answers to be the same? Why or why not?

d. Suppose you spin 300 times instead of 30 times. Do you expect your answers to become closer to or further from the fractions you found in part (b)? Explain your reasoning.

e. When you spin, is it equally likely that the pointer will land on red, on blue, or on yellow? Explain.

f. Suppose you use the spinner to play a game with a friend. Your friend scores a point every time the pointer lands on red. To make the game fair, for what outcomes should you score a point? Explain.

g. Suppose you use this spinner to play a three-person game. Player A scores if the pointer lands on yellow. Player B scores if the pointer lands on red. Player C scores if the pointer lands on blue. How can you assign points so that the game is fair?

2. The cooks at Kyla's school make the spinners below to help them choose the lunch menu. They let the students take turns spinning. For parts (a)–(c), decide which spinner you would choose. Explain your reasoning.

Spinner A   **Spinner B**

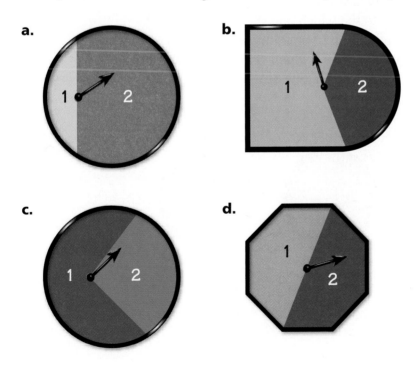

a. Your favorite lunch is pizza.

b. Your favorite lunch is lasagna.

c. Your favorite lunch is hot dogs.

3. When you use each of the spinners below, the two possible outcomes are landing on 1 and landing on 2. Are the outcomes equally likely? If not, which outcome has a greater theoretical probability? Explain.

a.

b.

c.

d.

4. A science club hosts a carnival to raise money. A game called Making Purple at the carnival involves using both of the spinners shown. If the player gets red on spinner A and blue on spinner B, the player wins because mixing red and blue makes purple.

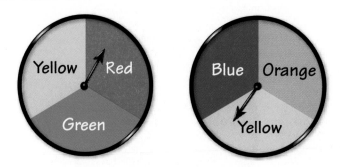

a. List the outcomes that are possible when you spin both pointers. Are these outcomes equally likely? Explain your reasoning.

b. What is the theoretical probability that a player "makes purple"? Explain.

c. If 100 people play the Making Purple game, how many people do you expect to win?

d. The club charges $1 per turn. A player who makes purple wins $5. Suppose 100 people play. How much money do you expect the club to make?

5. Molly designs a game for a class project. She makes the three spinners shown. She tests to see which one she likes best for her game. She spins each pointer 20 times and writes down her results, but she forgets to record which spinner gives which set of data. Match each spinner with one of the data sets. Explain your answer.

Homework Help Online
PHSchool.com

For: Help with Exercise 5
Web Code: ame-7305

Spinner A   Spinner B   Spinner C

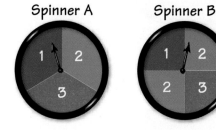 

First data set:	1, 2, 3, 2, 1, 1, 2, 1, 2, 2, 2, 3, 2, 1, 2, 2, 2, 3, 2, 2
Second data set:	2, 3, 1, 1, 3, 3, 3, 1, 1, 2, 3, 2, 2, 2, 1, 1, 1, 3, 3, 3
Third data set:	1, 2, 3, 3, 1, 2, 2, 2, 3, 2, 1, 2, 2, 2, 3, 2, 2, 3, 2, 1

6. Three people play a game on each spinner in Exercise 5. Player 1 scores a point if the pointer lands on 1. Player 2 scores a point if the pointer lands on 2. Player 3 scores a point if the pointer lands on 3.

   a. On which spinner(s) is the game a fair game? Why?

   b. Choose a spinner that you think doesn't make a fair game. Then, change the scoring rules to make the game fair by assigning different points for landing on the different numbers. Explain why your point system works.

7. **a.** Make a spinner and a set of rules for a fair two-person game. Explain why your game is fair.

   b. Make a spinner and a set of rules for a two-person game that is *not* fair. Explain why your game is not fair.

8. **Multiple Choice** Jake, Carl, and John try to decide what to do after school. Jake thinks they should play video games. Carl wants to see a movie. John thinks they should ride their bikes. Which choice is a fair way to decide?

   A. Let's toss three coins. If they all match, we play video games. If there are exactly two heads, we see a movie. If there are exactly two tails, we ride our bikes.

   B. Let's roll a number cube. If we roll a 1 or 2, we play video games. If we roll a 3 or 4, we go to the movies. Otherwise, we ride bikes.

   C. Let's use this spinner.

   D. None of these is fair.

9. **Multiple Choice** The Millers can't decide whether to eat pizza or burritos for dinner.

   F. Let's roll a number cube and toss a coin. If the number cube is even and the coin is heads, then we eat pizza. If the number cube is odd and the coin is tails, then we eat burritos. If neither happens, we try again.

   G. Let's toss a coin. If it is heads, we eat pizza. If it is tails, we do *not* eat burritos.

   H. Each of these is fair.

   J. Neither of these is fair.

10. Tawanda wants fewer winners for her scratch-off cards. She orders new cards with six spots. Two of the spots on each card match. What is the probability that a person who plays once will win on the card?

Connections

For Exercises 11–16, complete the following table. Write each probability as a fraction, decimal, or percent.

Probabilities

	Fraction	Decimal	Percent
11.	$\frac{1}{4}$	▩	25%
12.	$\frac{1}{8}$	▩	▩
13.	▩	▩	$33\frac{1}{3}$%
14.	▩	▩	10%
15.	▩	0.1666…	▩
16.	▩	0.05	▩

Go Online
PHSchool.com

For: Multiple-Choice Skills Practice
Web Code: ama-7354

17. The cooks at Kyla's school let students make spinners to determine the lunch menu.

a. Make a spinner for which the chance of lasagna is 25%, the chance of a hamburger is $16\frac{2}{3}$% and the chance of a tuna sandwich is $33\frac{1}{3}$%. The last choice is hot dogs.

b. What is the chance of hot dogs?

18. Three of the following situations have the same probability of getting "spinach." What is the probability for these three situations?

a. Spin the pointer on this spinner once.

b. Roll a number cube once. You get "spinach" when you roll a multiple of 3.

c. Toss two coins. You get "spinach" with one head and one tail.

d. Roll a number cube once. You get "spinach" when you roll a 5 or 6.

For Exercises 19–21, rewrite each pair of numbers. Insert <, >, or = to make a true statement.

19. $\dfrac{1}{3\frac{1}{2}}$ ■ $\dfrac{1}{4}$ **20.** $\dfrac{3.5}{7}$ ■ $\dfrac{1}{2}$ **21.** 0.30 ■ $\dfrac{1}{3}$

22. Use the table of historic baseball statistics to answer parts (a)–(d).

Batting Averages		
Player	**At Bats**	**Hits**
Nomar Garciaparra	4,089	1,317
Derek Jeter	5,457	1,715
Jackie Robinson	4,877	1,518

a. What percent of Nomar Garciaparra's at bats resulted in a hit?

b. What percent of Derek Jeter's at bats resulted in a hit?

c. What percent of Jackie Robinson's at bats resulted in a hit?

d. Suppose each player comes to bat today with the same skill his record shows. Who has the greatest chance of getting a hit? Explain.

For Exercises 23–25, rewrite each fraction as an equivalent fraction using a denominator of 10 or 100. Then, write a decimal number for each fraction.

23. $\dfrac{3}{20}$ **24.** $\dfrac{2}{5}$ **25.** $\dfrac{11}{25}$

26. A-1 Trucks used this graph to show that their trucks last longer than other trucks.

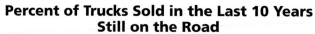
Percent of Trucks Sold in the Last 10 Years Still on the Road

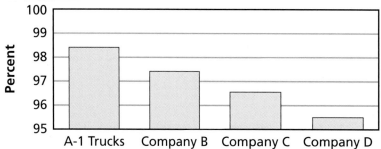

a. The bar for A-1 Trucks is about six times the height of Company D's bar. Does this mean that the chance of one of A-1's trucks lasting ten years is about six times as great as the chance of one of Company D's trucks lasting ten years? Explain.

b. If you wanted to buy a truck, would this graph convince you to buy a truck from A-1 Trucks? Why or why not?

27. The Federal Trade Commission (FTC) makes rules for businesses that buy and sell things. One rule states that an advertisement may be found unlawful if it can deceive a person.

To decide whether an ad is deceptive, the FTC considers the "general impression" it makes on a "reasonable person." Even if every statement is true, the ad is deceptive if it gives an overall false impression. For example, cows can't appear in margarine ads because it gives the false impression that margarine is a dairy product.

a. Tawanda places this ad in a newspaper. Qualifying customers receive a prize card like the ones described in the introduction to Problem 3.3. According to the FTC, is it legal for Tawanda to say, "Every card is a winner"? Explain.

b. Design a better ad that excites people but does not lead some to think they will win every time.

c. Find an ad that might be deceptive. Why do you think it is deceptive? What proof could the company provide to change your mind?

28. A sugarless gum company used to have an advertisement that stated:

> Four out of five dentists surveyed recommend sugarless gum for their patients who chew gum.

Do you think this statement means that 80% of dentists believe their patients should chew sugarless gum? Explain your reasoning.

29. Portland Middle School students make a flag as shown. After it hangs outside for a month, it looks dirty so they examine it. They find more bugs stuck on the yellow part than on the green part. Cheng says bugs are more attracted to yellow than to green.

a. Students in a science class test Cheng's conjecture with a design the same as the flag design. Suppose Cheng's conjecture is true. What is the chance that a bug landing at random on the flag hits the yellow part?

b. Suppose 13 bugs land on the yellow part and 12 bugs land on the green part. Is this evidence that supports Cheng's conjecture?

Pi can be estimated using probability. Take a square that is 2 units on each side and inscribe a circle inside which has a radius of 1 unit.

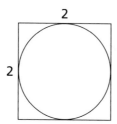

The area of the square is 4 square units and the area of the circle is $\pi \cdot r^2$ or $\pi \cdot 1^2 = \pi$ square units.

The ratio of the area of the circle to the area of the square is $\frac{\pi}{4}$. Ratios can be written as fractions.

Computer simulations can be done where the computer randomly places a dot inside the square. A computer can place 10,000 dots inside the square in less than 30 seconds.

This ratio $\dfrac{\text{number of dots inside the circle}}{\text{total number of dots inside the square}}$ should approximate $\frac{\pi}{4}$.

So, π should equal four times the ratio $\dfrac{\text{number of dots inside the circle}}{\text{total number of dots inside the square}}$.

30. Charlie runs three computer simulations such as the one described in the Did You Know? He records data for the three trials.

a. Complete the table below of Charlie's data.

Pi Estimations

Trial	Dots Inside the Circle	Dots Inside the Square	Ratio: $\dfrac{\text{Dots in Circle}}{\text{Dots in Square}}$
1	388	500	▨
2	352	450	▨
3	373	475	▨

b. Decide which trial is closest to an approximation for $\frac{\pi}{4}$. Explain your reasoning.

Extensions

31. Design a spinner with five regions so that the chances of landing in each region are equally likely. Give the number of degrees in the central angle of each region.

32. Design a spinner with five regions so that the chances of landing in one region are twice the chances of landing in each of the other four regions. Give the number of degrees in the central angle of each region.

For Exercises 33–35, design a contest for each company. Each contest should help the company attract customers, but not make the company lose money. Explain the rules, including any requirements for entering the contest.

33. The manager of a small clothing store wants to design a contest in which 1 of every 30 players wins a prize.

34. The director of operations for a chain of supermarkets wants to design a contest with a $100,000 grand prize!

35. An auto store sells new and used cars. The owner wants to have a contest with lots of winners and big prizes. She wants about one of every ten players to win a $500 prize.

Mathematical Reflections 3

In this investigation, you used spinners and cubes in probability situations. You used both experimental and theoretical probabilities to help you make decisions. These questions will help you summarize what you learned.

Think about your answers to these questions. Discuss your ideas with other students and your teacher. Then write a summary of your findings in your notebook.

1. Describe a situation in which you and a friend can use probability to make a decision. Can the probabilities of the outcomes be determined both experimentally and theoretically? Why or why not?

2. Describe a situation in which it is difficult or impossible to find the theoretical probabilities of the outcomes.

3. Explain what it means for a probability situation to be fair.

Investigation 4

Probability, Genetics, and Games

Have you ever heard of genes? (We don't mean the kind you wear!) What color are your eyes? Can you curl your tongue? Your birth parents gave you a unique set of genes that determine such things.

Scientists who study traits such as eye and hair color are called geneticists (juh NET uh sists). Geneticists use probability to predict certain traits in children based on traits in their parents or relatives.

4.1 Genetic Traits

Look at the earlobe of a classmate. Is it attached or does it dangle freely? The type of earlobe you have is a trait determined by your genes. Here is a description of four genetic traits:

- *Attached earlobe*: An earlobe is attached if its lowest point is attached directly to the head, as shown below.
- *Dimple*: A dimple is a small indentation, usually near the mouth.
- *Straight hair*: Straight hair has no waves or curls. (Note: Consider only how a person's hair is naturally.)
- *Widow's peak*: A widow's peak is a V-shaped hairline, as shown below.

Attached earlobe

Unattached earlobe

Widow's peak

No widow's peak

The table lists four genetic traits.

Classroom Genetics Survey

Trait	Yes	No	Total
Attached Earlobes	■	■	■
Dimples	■	■	■
Straight Hair	■	■	■
Widow's Peak	■	■	■

A. Copy the table. Find the number of people in your class who have each trait and record the results in your table.

B. Use your table to complete parts (1)–(4).

   1. For each trait, find the probability that a person chosen at random has the trait.

   2. What is the probability that a person chosen at random does *not* have straight hair?

   3. How many students in your school do you expect to have attached earlobes?

   4. How many students in your school do you expect to have a widow's peak?

C. Below are the results of a study of students from around the country.

U.S. Genetics Survey

Trait	Yes	No
Attached Earlobes	443	1,080
Dimples	445	1,066
Straight Hair	623	666
Widow's Peak	734	777

   1. Find the probability that a person chosen at random has each trait.

   2. How do the probabilities in Question B compare to the probabilities from the national data?

ACE Homework starts on page 62.

In the last problem, you looked at experimental probabilities for certain traits. In some cases, you can determine the probability that a child will have a trait based on his or her parents' genes.

Geneticists use the word *allele* (uh LEEL) for one of a pair of genes that determines a trait. For example, you have two alleles that determine whether your earlobes are attached. You receive one of these alleles from your birth mother and one from your birth father. Of course, each parent has two earlobe alleles.

Let's use *e* to represent the allele for attached earlobes. Let *E* represent the allele for nonattached earlobes. If you receive an *e* allele from each parent, your earlobe alleles will be *ee*, and you will have attached earlobes. If you receive an *E* allele from each parent, your earlobe alleles will be *EE*. Then you will have nonattached earlobes.

What if you receive one *E* and one *e* allele? In nature, the *E* allele is *dominant* and the *e* allele is *recessive*. This means that you have an *Ee* combination, the *E* dominates, and you will have nonattached earlobes.

Earlobe Alleles

Letters	Earlobe Trait
EE	Nonattached
Ee or *eE*	Nonattached
ee	Attached

An Example: Bonnie and Evan's Baby

Bonnie and Evan are going to have a baby. Bonnie's earlobe alleles are *Ee*, and Evan's earlobe alleles are *ee*. You can determine the probability that their baby will have attached earlobes by making a tree diagram.

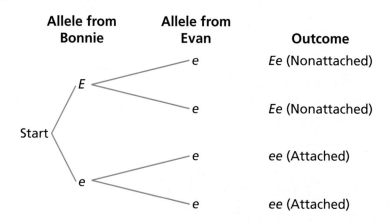

There are four possible allele pairs (outcomes). Two of these pairs, *ee* and *ee*, result in attached earlobes. The probability that Bonnie and Evan's baby will have attached earlobes is $\frac{2}{4}$, or $\frac{1}{2}$.

You can also find the probabilities by making a table such as the one at the right. List Evan's alleles along the side and Bonnie's alleles on top. The four white squares show the possible combinations.

		Bonnie	
		E	**e**
Evan	e	Ee	ee
	e	Ee	ee

Bonnie and Evan's chart is sometimes called a *Punnett square* by geneticists. A Punnett square is a chart which predicts all possible gene combinations. Punnett squares are named for an English geneticist, Reginald Punnett. He discovered some basic principles of genetics. He studied the feather color traits of chickens in order to quickly determine whether chickens were male or female when they were born.

Go Online
PHSchool.com **For:** Information about Punnett squares
Web Code: ame-9031

In Questions A–C, examine each family situation and answer the questions.

A. Dasan's mother is expecting her third child. His mother and father both have the earlobe alleles *Ee*.

    1. What is the probability that Dasan's new sibling will have attached earlobes?

    2. What is the probability that his new sibling will have nonattached earlobes?

B. Geoff's earlobe alleles are *EE* and Mali's earlobe alleles are *Ee*. What is the probability that their child will have nonattached earlobes?

C. Both of Eileen's parents have attached earlobes. What is the probability that Eileen has attached earlobes?

 **Homework starts on page 62.**

There are many other traits you can study in the way you studied earlobes. For example, having certain characteristics (dimples, curly or wavy hair, and widow's peak) is dominant over not having the characteristics.

Did You Know?

There are dominant traits that do not show up very often in the population. For example, the trait for six fingers on one hand is a dominant trait, and five fingers is a recessive trait. Because only a few people carry the allele for six fingers, very few people are born with this trait.

Greg Harris, a major-league baseball player from 1981 to 1995, has six fingers on one hand. He had a specially designed, reversible six-fingered glove. In 1995, he became the only pitcher since 1900 to pitch with both hands in a major-league game.

Go Online
PHSchool.com
For: Information about genetic traits
Web Code: ame-9031

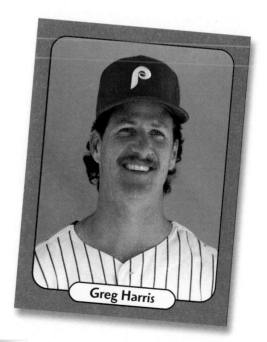
Greg Harris

Have you ever figured out a strategy for winning a game?

Now that you know about making tables and diagrams to find probabilities, you can use these tools to find winning strategies for games. In this problem, you play a two-team game called Roller Derby.

Each team needs a game board with columns numbered 1–12, a pair of number cubes, and 12 markers (such as coins, buttons, or small blocks).

Roller Derby Rules

1. Each team places its 12 markers into their columns in any way it chooses.

2. Each team rolls a number cube. The team with the highest roll goes first.

3. Teams take turns rolling the two number cubes. They remove a marker from the column on their board with the same number as the total sum of the numbers on the number cubes. If the column is empty, the team does not get to remove a marker.

4. The first team to remove all the markers from its board wins.

As you play, think about strategies for winning and how probability relates to your strategies.

Problem 4.3 Analyzing a Game

A. Play the game at least twice. For each game, record the strategies you use to place your markers on the board. Also, record how many times each sum is rolled. What is a good strategy for placing your markers on the game board?

B. 1. Which sums seem to occur most often?

   2. Which sums do not come up very often?

C. Find all the possible outcomes (number pairs) of rolling two number cubes. Find the sums for each of these outcomes.

   1. Are all the sums equally likely? Explain.

   2. How many ways can you get a sum of 2?

   3. What is the probability of getting a sum of 4?

   4. What is the probability of getting a sum of 6?

   5. Which sums occur most often?

D. Now that you have looked at the possible outcomes of the Roller Derby game, do you have any new strategies for winning? Explain.

ACE Homework starts on page 62.

Did You Know?

Galileo was an Italian physicist, astronomer, and mathematician. He is famous for helping develop a model in which the sun was the center of the universe. He also studied problems in probability similar to the ones you have seen.

A famous problem he worked on involved rolling three number cubes. He looked at the possibilities for getting a sum of 9 or a sum of 10. A sum of 9 is made using six groups of numbers:

$$(1, 2, 6), (1, 3, 5), (1, 4, 4), (2, 2, 5), (2, 3, 4), \text{ and } (3, 3, 3).$$

A sum of 10 is made using six other groups of numbers:

$$(1, 3, 6), (1, 4, 5), (2, 2, 6), (2, 3, 5), (2, 4, 4), \text{ and } (3, 3, 4).$$

What puzzled people is that, when they did experiments, the sum of 10 occurred more often. By making a diagram similar to a counting tree, Galileo showed the theoretical probability matched the experimental results. There are actually 25 combinations that have a sum of 9 and 27 combinations that have a sum of 10.

For: Information about Galileo
Web Code: ame-9031

Applications

1. A foot arch is a genetic trait. A foot arch is a space between the middle of a person's foot and the floor when the person stands. In a national study, 982 people said they had a foot arch, while 445 people said they did not have a foot arch.

   a. Based on these data, what is the experimental probability that a person chosen at random has a foot arch?

   b. In a recent year, about 16,600 people participated in the Boston Marathon. Use the data above to estimate the number of participants who did *not* have a foot arch. Explain.

   c. If you know people who are runners, find out if they have foot arches. Does your data seem to match the national study data?

2. Some genetic traits are gender-linked. These traits are more prevalent in people of one gender than the other. For example, color blindness is far more common in men than in women. About 7% of the U.S. male population either cannot distinguish red from green, or sees red and green differently from most people. Red-green color blindness only affects about 0.4% of U.S. females.

   About 550 males and 600 females attend a middle school. How many males and females do you predict have red-green color blindness?

For Exercises 3–7, use the following information about the genetics of tongue curling to answer the question.

Let *T* stand for the allele for tongue curling and let *t* stand for the allele for non-curling. *T* is dominant, so people with *TT* or *Tt* can curl their tongues, while people with *tt* cannot.

3. Neither Greg nor Megan can curl their tongues. What is the probability that their daughter can curl her tongue? Explain.

4. Suppose a woman with tongue-curling alleles *TT* and her husband with tongue-curling alleles *tt* are expecting a baby. What is the probability that the baby will be able to curl his tongue? Explain.

5. If Laura can curl her tongue, is it possible that neither of her parents can curl their tongues? Why or why not?

6. Suppose Ryan can't curl his tongue. Is it possible that both of his parents can curl their tongues? Why or why not?

7. Suppose both Niran and Gen can curl their tongues. They are wondering how many of their children will have this ability.

   a. Gen's mother can curl her tongue, but her father can't. What are Gen's tongue-curling alleles? Explain.

   b. Niran's mother can't curl her tongue, but his father can. What are Niran's tongue-curling alleles? Explain.

   c. What is the probability that Niran and Gen's first child will have the tongue-curling ability?

   d. Suppose their first child has the tongue-curling ability. What is the probability that their second child will also have this ability?

   e. Suppose Niran and Gen have ten children. How many of their children would you expect to have the tongue-curling ability? Why?

8. What is the probability of getting a sum of 5 when you roll two number cubes?

   A. $\frac{1}{9}$ **B.** $\frac{1}{6}$ **C.** $\frac{1}{4}$ **D.** $\frac{1}{3}$

9. What is the probability of getting a sum greater than 9 when you roll two number cubes?

   F. $\frac{1}{9}$ **G.** $\frac{1}{6}$ **H.** $\frac{1}{4}$ **J.** $\frac{1}{3}$

Multiple Choice For Exercises 10 and 11, Ella is playing Roller Derby with Carlos. Ella places all her markers in column 1 and Carlos places all of his markers in column 12.

10. What is the probability that Ella will win?

    A. 0   **B.** $\frac{1}{3}$ **C.** $\frac{1}{2}$ **D.** 1

11. What is the probability that Carlos will win?

    F. 0   **G.** $\frac{1}{3}$ **H.** $\frac{1}{2}$ **J.** 1

12. In some board games, you can end up in "jail." One way to get out of jail is to roll doubles (two number cubes that match). What is the probability of getting out of jail on your turn by rolling doubles? Use your list of possible outcomes of rolling two number cubes. Explain your reasoning.

For: Help with Exercise 12
Web Code: ame-7412

Connections

For Exercises 13–17, use the data below to answer the question. If there is not enough information to answer the question, explain what additional information you need.

Careers and Goals for Young People		
Career/Goal	Ages 8–12	Ages 13–21
Be a millionaire	65%	65%
Star in movie/TV	34%	47%
Make movies	32%	43%
Be a famous athlete	32%	24%
Be a musician/singer	28%	46%
Cure a disease	27%	43%
Start a big company	22%	37%
Be President of the United States	22%	18%
Be a famous writer	22%	33%
Win a Nobel Prize	20%	28%

SOURCE: *Harris Interactive Youthpulse*

13. Which group is more likely to want to be a musician/singer?

14. In a group of 1,500 young people (ages 13–21), about how many would choose to cure a disease?

15. Order the five lowest career/goal choices from least to greatest for ages 13–21.

16. About how many people in your school would select famous athlete as a career?

17. In order to find the percent of all young people (ages 8–12) who want to star in a movie/TV or make a movie, can you add the percents for the two careers/goals together? Why or why not?

18. Suppose you try to determine Fia's and Tomas's earlobe alleles. Here is the information you have:

- Fia has attached earlobes.
- Tomas has nonattached earlobes.
- Their two daughters have nonattached earlobes.
- Their son has attached earlobes.

a. What are Fia's earlobe alleles?

b. What are Tomas's earlobe alleles?

c. If they have another child, what is the probability that the child will have attached earlobes?

19. In *Shapes and Designs*, you built triangles and parallelograms with a given set of criteria. You know that sometimes two people can construct different geometric shapes, given the same set of directions.

a. Suppose your teacher tells you the lengths of all three sides of a given triangle. What is the probability that you construct a triangle congruent to the one that your teacher has in mind? Explain.

b. Suppose your teacher tells you the lengths of all four sides of a given parallelogram. What is the probability that you construct a parallelogram congruent to the parallelogram that your teacher has in mind? Explain.

c. Suppose your teacher tells you the lengths of all four sides of a given rectangle. What is the probability that you construct a rectangle congruent to the one that your teacher has in mind? Explain.

d. Suppose your teacher tells you the perimeter of a given rectangle. What is the probability that you construct a rectangle congruent to the one that your teacher has in mind?

e. Suppose your teacher tells you the lengths of all four sides and the area of a given parallelogram. What is the probability that you construct a parallelogram congruent to the one that your teacher has in mind?

For Exercises 20–23, use your list of possible outcomes when you roll two number cubes to help you answer the questions.

20. What is the probability that the sum is a multiple of 4?

21. What is the probability that the sum is a common multiple of 2 and 3?

22. What is the probability that the sum is a prime number? Explain.

23. Which has a greater probability of being rolled on a pair of number cubes, a sum that is a factor of 6 or a sum that is a multiple of 6? Explain.

24. Suppose Jose and Nina play the game Evens and Odds. To play the game, they roll two number cubes and find the product of the numbers. If the product is odd, Nina scores a point. If the product is even, Jose scores a point.

  a. Make a table of the possible products of two number cubes.

  b. What is the probability that Nina wins? What is the probability that Jose wins? Explain your reasoning.

  c. Is this a fair game? If not, how could you change the points scored by each player so that it would be fair?

  d. What is the probability that the product is a prime number?

  e. What is the probability that the product is a factor of 4?

25. Aran knows that if you roll a number cube once, there is a 50% chance of getting an even number. He says that if you roll a number cube twice, the chance of getting at least one even number is doubled. Is he correct?

26. a. Suppose you fold this shape along the dashed lines to make a three-dimensional shape. How many faces will it have?

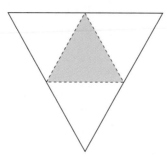

b. Suppose you roll the shape in part (a). What is the probability that the shaded face lands on the bottom?

c. Suppose you fold the shape below. Can you use it in a game? Will the game be fair? Explain.

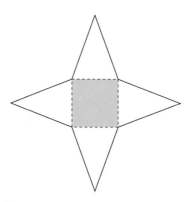

Extensions

27. Pick one of the following two options:

a. Investigate the earlobes in your family. Make a family tree that shows the earlobe alleles that you can find for each person. Trace back as many generations as you can.

b. Survey a large number of people to estimate the percentage of people in the population who have attached earlobes. Represent the data in a graph.

Mathematical Reflections 4

In this investigation, you explored probability related to genetics and games. You collected data to determine the probability that a person selected at random would have a genetic trait. You also found the probability that a child would have a trait based on information about his or her parents' genes. You examined a game to determine winning strategies for playing the game. These questions will help you summarize what you have learned.

Think about your answers to these questions. Discuss your ideas with other students and your teacher. Then write a summary of your findings in your notebook.

1. How can you collect the data to find the experimental probability that a person chosen at random from your school has a particular trait?

2. Describe a way you can find the theoretical probability that a baby will have a trait, such as attached earlobes or tongue-curling ability. Base your answer on the alleles of the parents.

3. Describe some of the strategies for determining the theoretical probabilities for situations in this unit. Give an example of a situation for each of the strategies.

Looking Back and Looking Ahead

Unit Review

The problems in this unit explored some of the big ideas in probability. You learned

- how to think about chance in activities for which individual trials have uncertain outcomes, but patterns of outcomes emerge after many trials

- how to use experimental and theoretical probabilities to predict outcomes with number cubes or coins

- that some outcomes are equally likely while others are not

- how to analyze games of chance to determine whether they are fair games

Go Online
PHSchool.com

For: Vocabulary Review Puzzle
Web Code: amj-7051

Use Your Understanding: Probability

Test your understanding of probability by solving the following problems.

1. Joanna designs a game for the school carnival. She prepares two bags of marbles.

   To play the game, a contestant selects one marble from each bag. If the colors of the marbles match, the contestant wins a prize.

   a. These are the win/loss results for the first 30 games.

W	L	L	W	W	L	L	W	W	L	L	W
W	L	L	L	W	L	L	L	L	W	L	W
L	L	L	L	W	W						

   What do these data tell you about the experimental probability of winning the game?

   b. What is the theoretical probability of winning the game?

   c. What explains the difference between your answers to parts (a) and (b)?

Bag A

Bag B

70 How Likely Is It?

2. Kiana designs a number-cube game for a carnival. To play the game, a contestant rolls two number cubes. If the greatest common factor of the two numbers rolled is even, the contestant wins a prize.

    a. Describe how to conduct an experiment to find the experimental probability of winning the game. Include how you would record results and use them to find experimental probabilities.

    b. What is the theoretical probability of winning the game?

    c. Is this a fair game? Explain your reasoning.

Explain Your Reasoning

3. Consider activities with uncertain outcomes like games of chance or genetic inheritance.

    a. How do you find experimental probabilities for the possible outcomes?

    b. How do you find theoretical probabilities for the possible outcomes?

    c. What relationship do you expect between experimental and theoretical probabilities for any event if the experimental probability is based on each of the following number of trials?

        i. 5   **ii.** 50   **iii.** 500

4. Explain the relationship between equally likely and fair when playing a game of chance.

5. What does it mean when a set of outcomes is *not* equally likely? Give an example.

6. For Question 1, suppose Joanna charges $5 to play her game and you can win $10 if you select a marble from each bag and they match. How can you use probability to decide if you want to play the game or not?

Look Ahead

The ideas of probability will be used and developed further in several other units of *Connected Mathematics*, especially *What Do You Expect?* You will also find that you can apply probability reasoning in areas of science, personal health care, safety, and games of chance.

English/Spanish Glossary

C

certain outcome A result of an action or event that is certain to happen. For example, the sun will rise tomorrow (even if it stays behind clouds all day). The probability of a certain outcome is 1.

suceso seguro Resultado de una acción o suceso que ocurrirá. Por ejemplo, el sol saldrá mañana (incluso si hay nubes). La probabilidad de ese resultado es 1.

chance The likelihood that something will happen. Chance is often expressed as a percent. For example, a weather forecaster might say that there is a 30% chance that it will rain tomorrow.

posibilidad Probabilidad de que algo ocurra. La posibilidad se expresa como un porcentaje. Por ejemplo, un metereólogo puede decir que hay un 30% de probabilidad de que llueva mañana.

E

equally likely events Two or more events that have the same chance of happening. For example, when you toss a fair coin, heads and tails are equally likely. Each has a 50% chance of happening. When you toss a tack, it is not equally likely to land on its side and on its head. It is more likely to land on its side.

sucesos igualmente probables Dos o más sucesos que tienen las mismas posibilidades de suceder. Por ejemplo, cuando lanzas una moneda "justa," la probabilidad de que salga cara o cruz es igualmente probable. Cada resultado tiene una probabilidad del 50% de que suceda. Cuando tiras una tachuela, no existe la misma probabilidad de que caiga sobre un lado que de cabeza. Es más probable que caiga de lado.

event A set of outcomes. For example, when you toss two coins, getting two matching coins is an event consisting of the outcomes heads-heads (HH) and tails-tails (TT).

suceso Un conjunto de resultados. Por ejemplo, cuando se lanzan dos monedas, lograr que las dos monedas coincidan es un suceso que consiste en los resultados cara-cara (CC) y cruz-cruz (XX).

experimental probability A probability found as a result of an experiment. Experimental probabilities are used to predict behavior over the long run. For example, you could find the experimental probability of getting heads when you toss a coin by tossing the coin several times and keeping track of the outcomes. The experimental probability would be the relative frequency of heads, that is the ratio of the number of heads to the total number of trials.

probabilidad experimental Una probabilidad hallada mediante la experimentación. Las probabilidades experimentales se usan para predecir lo que podría suceder con el tiempo. Por ejemplo, podrías hallar la probabilidad experimental de que salgan caras cuando lanzas una moneda varias veces, si llevas la cuenta de los resultados. La probabilidad experimental sería la frecuencia relativa de que salgan caras, que es la razón del número de caras sobre el total del número de pruebas.

fair game A game is fair when each player has the same chance of winning. A game that is not fair can be made fair by adjusting the pay-offs (or scoring system). For example, suppose you play a game in which two coins are tossed. You score when the coins both land heads up. Otherwise, your opponent scores. The probability that you will score is $\frac{1}{4}$ and the probability that your opponent will score is $\frac{3}{4}$. To make the game fair, you must get three points each time you score, and your opponent must get only one point when he scores. A coin is fair when the probability of tossing a head equals the probability of tossing a tail.

juego justo Un juego en el que cada jugador tiene las mismas posibilidades de ganar. Un juego que no es justo se puede hacer justo mediante una adaptación del sistema de resultados. Por ejemplo, supón que juegas a tirar dos monedas. Obtienes un punto cuando las dos monedas caen cara arriba. Si no, tu oponente recibe un punto. La probabilidad de que consigas el punto es $\frac{1}{4}$ y la probabilidad de que tu oponente consiga un punto es $\frac{3}{4}$. Para hacer que el juego sea justo, deberás obtener tres puntos cada vez que las dos monedas caigan cara arriba y tu oponente deberá obtener un punto cuando las monedas caigan de otro modo. El juego de la moneda es justo cuando la probabilidad de que caiga en cara es igual a la probabilidad de que caiga en cruz.

favorable outcome An outcome that gives a desired result. A favorable outcome is sometimes called a *success*. For example, when you toss two coins to find the probability of the coins matching, HH and TT are favorable outcomes.

resultado favorable Un resultado en el que estás interesado. A veces, un resultado favorable se llama un *éxito*. Por ejemplo, cuando lanzas dos monedas para hallar la probabilidad de que las dos coincidan, los resultados CC y XX son resultados favorables.

impossible outcome An outcome that cannot happen. For example, the probability of getting a 7 by tossing a number cube is zero. We write $P(7) = 0$.

suceso imposible Un suceso que no puede ocurrir. Por ejemplo, la probabilidad de obtener un 7 al lanzar un cubo numérico es cero. Se escribe $P(7) = 0$.

outcome A possible result of an action. For example, when one number cube is rolled, the possible outcomes are 1, 2, 3, 4, 5, and 6.

resultado Lo que sucede como consecuencia o efecto de una acción. Por ejemplo, cuando se lanza un cubo numerado, los resultados posibles son 1, 2, 3, 4, 5 y 6.

possible A word used to describe an outcome or result that can happen. *Possible* does not imply anything about how likely the outcome is. For example, it is *possible* to toss a coin 200 times and get heads every time, but it is not at all likely.

posible Una palabra usada para describir un suceso que puede ocurrir. *Posible* no implica nada sobre la probabilidad de que suceda. Por ejemplo, es *posible* lanzar una moneda 200 veces y que salgan caras todas las veces pero no es nada probable.

probability A number with a value from 0 to 1 that describes the likelihood that an event will occur. For example, if a bag contains a red marble, a white marble, and a blue marble, then the probability of selecting a red marble is $\frac{1}{3}$.

probabilidad Un número entre 0 y 1 que describe la posibilidad de que un suceso ocurra. Por ejemplo, si una bolsa contiene una canica roja, una blanca y una azul, entonces la probabilidad de sacar una canica roja es $\frac{1}{3}$.

probable Another way to say *likely*. An outcome that is probable is likely to happen.

probable Otra manera de decir *posible*. Un resultado posible que seguramente ocurrirá.

random events Events for which the outcome is uncertain when they are viewed as individual events. Random events often exhibit a regular pattern when observed over many trials. For example, when you roll a number cube, the number that will result is uncertain on any one particular roll, but over a great many rolls each number will occur about the same number of times.

sucesos aleatorios Sucesos que no son seguros individualmente, pero que podrían exhibir un patrón regular cuando son observados a lo largo de muchas pruebas. Por ejemplo, cuando lanzas un cubo numerado, no hay ninguna manera de saber el resultado del próximo tiro, pero sabes que con el tiempo cada número saldrá aproximadamente la misma cantidad de veces.

simulation A model of an experiment used to find the likelihood of an event. For example, suppose you want to find the likelihood you will win a contest with ten contestants. Since it is difficult to gather information about the contestants, you can simulate the contest. Write the numbers 1–10 on cards and select a card at random. The number 1 represents a win and the numbers 2–10 represent a loss.

simulación Modelo de un experimento que se usa para hallar la probabilidad de un suceso. Por ejemplo, supón que quieres saber la probabilidad que tendrás de ganar un concurso con diez participantes. Como es difícil reunir información sobre los participantes, puedes simular el concurso. Escribe los números 1–10 en tarjetas y selecciona una tarjeta al azar. El número 1 representa una ganancia y los números 2–10 representa una pérdida.

theoretical probability A probability found by analyzing a situation. If all the outcomes are equally likely, you can find a theoretical probability of an event by first listing all the possible outcomes, and then finding the ratio of the number of outcomes you are interested in to the total number of outcomes. For example, there are 36 possible equally likely outcomes (number pairs) when two number cubes are rolled. Of these outcomes, 6 have a sum of 7, so the probability of rolling a sum of 7 is $\frac{6}{36}$, or $\frac{1}{6}$.

probabilidad teórica Una probabilidad hallada mediante el análisis de una situación. Si todos los resultados son igualmente probables, puedes hallar una probabilidad teórica de un suceso haciendo primero una lista de todos los resultados posibles y luego hallando la razón entre el número de resultados en los que estás interesado y el número total de resultados. Por ejemplo, hay 36 resultados (pares de números) posibles e igualmente probables cuando se lanzan dos cubos numerados. De estos resultados, 6 tienen una suma de 7, así que la probabilidad de lanzar una suma de 7 es $\frac{6}{36}$ ó $\frac{1}{6}$.

tree diagram A systematic way to find all the possible outcomes in a probability situation.

diagrama de árbol Manera sistemática de hallar todos los resultados posibles en una probabilidad.

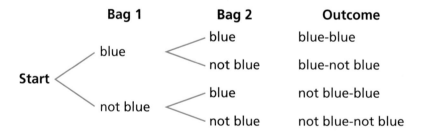

trial One round of an experiment. For example, if you are interested in the behavior of a coin, you might experiment by tossing a coin 50 times and recording the results. Each toss is a trial, so this experiment consists of 50 trials.

prueba Una parte en un experimento. Por ejemplo, si te interesan los resultados de tirar una moneda, puedes lanzarla al aire 50 veces y anotar los resultados. Cada lanzamiento es una prueba, por lo que este experimento consistiría en 50 pruebas.

Academic Vocabulary

The following terms are important to your understanding of the mathematics in this unit. Knowing and using these words will help you in thinking, reasoning, representing, communicating your ideas, and making connections across ideas. When these words make sense to you, the investigations and problems will make more sense as well.

D

design To make using specific criteria
related terms: draw, plan, outline, model

Sample: Carlos noticed that he gets home from school first about $\frac{1}{3}$ of the time, his brother gets home first about $\frac{1}{2}$ of the time, and his sister is first about $\frac{1}{6}$ of the time. Design a spinner to predict who will get home first tomorrow.

I designed a spinner with six equal sections. Three sixths or $\frac{1}{2}$ of these sections are labeled brother, two sixths or $\frac{1}{3}$ of them are labeled Carlos, and $\frac{1}{6}$ is labeled sister.

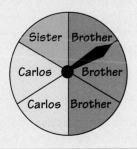

diseñar Hacer algo usando criterios específicos.
términos relacionados: dibujar, hacer un plan, hacer un esquema, hacer modelos

Ejemplo: Carlos observó que llega a casa de la escuela primero alrededor de $\frac{1}{3}$ del tiempo, su hermano llega a casa primero alrededor de $\frac{1}{2}$ del tiempo y su hermana llega primero alrededor de $\frac{1}{6}$ del tiempo. Diseña una flecha giratoria para predecir quién llegará primero a casa mañana.

Diseñé una flecha giratoria con seis secciones iguales. Tres sextos ó $\frac{1}{2}$ de estas secciones se rotularon hermano, dos sextos ó $\frac{1}{3}$ se rotularon Carlos y $\frac{1}{6}$ se rotuló hermana.

E

expect Using theoretical or experimental data to anticipate a certain outcome.
related terms: anticipate, predict

Sample: Lizzie and her sister flip a coin every afternoon to see who will walk the dog. How often should Lizzie expect to walk the dog?

There are two possible outcomes: heads or tails. The probability of heads or tails is $\frac{1}{2}$. Lizzie should expect to walk the dog half of the time.

esperar Usar datos teóricos o experimentales para anticipar un determinado resultado.
términos relacionados: anticipar, predecir

Ejemplo: Lizzie y su hermana lanzan una moneda cada tarde para ver quién sacará a pasear al perro. ¿Con cuánta frecuencia debería esperar Lizzie sacar a pasear al perro?

Hay dos resultados posibles: cara o cruz. La probabilidad de que caiga cara o cruz es la misma, $\frac{1}{2}$. Lizzie debería esperar sacar a pasear al perro la mitad del tiempo.

explain To give facts and details that make an idea easier to understand. Explaining can involve a written summary supported by a diagram, chart, table, or a combination of these.

related terms: clarify, describe, justify

Sample: **Ellen made a spinner to choose an exercise activity. Which do you think will occur most often? Explain your reasoning.**

Exercise Spinner

☐ Run
☐ Swim
☐ Bike

> Ellen is most likely to go for a run since the run portion of the spinner is the largest. It takes up $\frac{1}{2}$ of the spinner, while swim takes up only $\frac{1}{3}$ of the spinner and bike takes up $\frac{1}{6}$ of the spinner.

explicar Dar hechos y detalles que hacen que una idea sea más fácil de comprender. Explicar puede implicar un resumen escrito apoyado por hechos, un diagrama, una gráfica, una tabla o una combinación de éstos.

términos relacionados: aclarar, describir, justificar

Ejemplo: **Ellen hizo una flecha giratoria para elegir una actividad de ejercicio. ¿Cuál piensas que ocurrirá con mayor frecuencia? Explica tu razonamiento.**

Flecha Giratoria de Ejercicio

☐ Correr
☐ Nadar
☐ Andar en bicicleta

> Es más probable que Ellen salga a correr puesto que la porción de correr de la flecha es la más grande. Ocupa la $\frac{1}{2}$ de la flecha, mientras nadar ocupa sólo $\frac{1}{3}$ de la flecha y andar en bicicleta ocupa $\frac{1}{6}$ de la flecha.

P

predict To make an educated guess.

related terms: anticipate, expect, estimate

Sample: **Eli and Jake put colored crayons in a bag. Then they conducted an experiment to find the probability of pulling a green crayon out of the bag.**

Eli: *P*(green) = $\frac{10}{45}$

Jake: *P*(green) = $\frac{5}{12}$

Whose results would you use to best predict the likelihood of pulling a green crayon out of the bag?

> I would use Eli's results since he conducted the experiment more times than Jake did. The more often an experiment is repeated, the better the results are as a predictor of a future similar event.

predecir Hacer una estimación informada.

términos relacionados: anticipar, esperar, estimar

Ejemplo: **Eli y Jake pusieron creyones de colores en una bolsa. Luego realizaron un experimento para hallar la probabilidad de sacar un creyón verde de la bolsa.**

Eli: *P*(verde) = $\frac{10}{45}$

Jake: *P*(verde) = $\frac{5}{12}$

¿Los resultados de quién usarías para predecir mejor la probabilidad de sacar un creyón verde de la bolsa?

> Usaría los resultados de Eli puesto que realizó el experimento más veces que Jake. Entre más se repite un experimento, son mejores los resultados como pronosticador de un evento futuro similar.

Index

Acknowledgments

Team Credits

The people who made up the **Connected Mathematics2** team—representing editorial, editorial services, design services, and production services—are listed below. Bold type denotes core team members.

Leora Adler, Judith Buice, Kerry Cashman, Patrick Culleton, Sheila DeFazio, Richard Heater, **Barbara Hollingdale, Jayne Holman,** Karen Holtzman, **Etta Jacobs,** Christine Lee, Carolyn Lock, Catherine Maglio, **Dotti Marshall,** Rich McMahon, Eve Melnechuk, Kristin Mingrone, Terri Mitchell, **Marsha Novak,** Irene Rubin, Donna Russo, Robin Samper, Siri Schwartzman, **Nancy Smith,** Emily Soltanoff, **Mark Tricca,** Paula Vergith, Roberta Warshaw, Helen Young

Additional Credits

Diana Bonfilio, Mairead Reddin, Michael Torocsik, nSight, Inc.

Illustration

Michelle Barbera: 6

Technical Illustration

WestWords, Inc.

Cover Design

tom white.images

Photos

2 t, Russ Lappa; **2 b,** Michael Newman/PhotoEdit; **3,** Thinkstock/Getty Images, Inc.; **5,** Comstock Images/Getty Images, Inc.; **9 all,** Russ Lappa; **10,** ©1999 Scott Adams/Distributed by United Features Syndicate, Inc.; **12,** Camille Tokerud/Getty Images, Inc.; **14,** Richard Haynes; **19,** Gail Mooney/Masterfile; **21,** Jim Cummins/Getty Images, Inc.; **22,** Russ Lappa; **25,** Richard Haynes; **27,** Russ Lappa; **28,** Brian Hagiwara/Brand X Pictures/Getty Images, Inc.; **33,** Bob Daemmrich/PhotoEdit; **36,** Mark Scott/Getty Images, Inc.; **39,** David Young-Wolff/PhotoEdit; **41,** Gabe Palmer/Corbis; **42,** Michael Prince/Corbis; **55 l,** Corbis; **55 ml,** Alain Dex/Photo Researchers, Inc.; **55 mr,** David Young-Wolf/PhotoEdit; **55 r,** Michael Newman/PhotoEdit; **57,** Sarma Ozols/Getty Images, Inc.; **59,** AP/Wide World Photos; **62,** John Coletti/Index Stock Imagery, Inc.; **63,** Michael Newman/PhotoEdit; **64,** David Young-Wolff/PhotoEdit; **67,** Richard Haynes

Data Sources

The table of batting averages on page 49 is adapted from Major League Baseball Historical Player Statistics. Copyright © Major League Baseball.

The table "US Genetic Survey" on page 56 is from "The Genetics Project: Are We Alike?" Used with permission Dr. Jacalyn Willis, Director of PRISM, Montclair State University, Montclair, New Jersey.

Careers data on page 65 from The Harris Poll ® "Careers in the Arts (Coupled with Fame) Are High in Young People's Aspirations" Harris Interactive, Inc. All Rights Reserved.

Note: Every effort has been made to locate the copyright owner of the material reprinted in this book. Omissions brought to our attention will be corrected in subsequent editions.